CW01466974

2009 Poetry Competition for

YoungWriters

I have a dream 2009
Words to change the world

Martin Luther King

John Lennon

Southern England
Edited by Vivien Linton

Foreword

'I Have a Dream 2009' is a series of poetry
collections written by 11 to 18-year-olds from
schools and colleges across the UK and
overseas. Pupils were invited to send us their
poems using the theme 'I Have a Dream'.
Selected entries range from dreams they've
experienced to childhood fantasies of stardom
and wealth, through inspirational poems of
their dreams for a better future and of people
who have influenced and inspired their lives.

The series is a snapshot of who and what
inspires, influences and enthuses young
adults of today. It shows an insight into their
hopes, dreams and aspirations of the future
and displays how their dreams are an escape
from the pressures of today's modern life.
Young Writers are proud to present this
anthology, which is truly inspired and sure to
be an inspiration to all who read it.

Contents

Westergate Community School, Chichester

West Lodge First & Middle School, Pinner

Wood Green School, Witney

Wychwood School, Oxford

The Poems

My Mum

My mum is so lovely
She shines brighter than the sun
She fills my world with happiness
She is number one.

If she was a superhero
She would be the best one around
Taking care of everyone
Who gets stressed out.

My mum is so caring
She always puts me first
Without her personality
My bubble would burst.

My mum is the best
She is very wise
You can count on her
99% of the time.

I know she loves me
And I love her too
She's like a beautiful flower
Ready to bloom.

A daffodil for her sunny smile
Which brightens up my day
And a tulip for her kindness
For the things she does and says.

I am inspired by my mum so much
I just wanted her to know
And the whole wide world
In case they already didn't know.

Georgie Hopson (13)
Barnhill Community High School, Hayes

Dark Saviour

I have a dream about you; recurring bliss.
You're deadly, you're poison,
I shouldn't be with you
But something is drawing me in
What is it?
Your grasp is unbreakable
But my wish is not to break it
I just want you
My dark saviour.

Keep holding me
Never let me go
Let's just fly away together
Just you and me
Trying to change my mind won't work
You've put me in too deep
The secrets you never should have told
Are burned in my heart for all eternity.

The way you stare at me
With such cold eyes
Should turn me away
But only draws me in closer
You're the love
I never thought I would have
The way you smile
Your lips being that sweet venom
It makes me weak
I can't bear to look at you
Why you put up with me
I will never know
I will never understand you

Your mind works so much more differently
You are careful with your actions
You don't want to hurt me
I try to understand why,
Do you feel the same way?
Do you feel that love?
This is only wishful thinking

This is the dream I have every night.
Here you come again
Staring with those eyes,
Here you come again
My dark saviour.

Penny Kooner (14)
Barnhill Community High School, Hayes

She Was Dreaming . . .

She lay in her bed, gazing at the ceiling,
Wondering why she was feeling
So worthless and unappealing.

She did nothing significant for the world.
Nothing, she thought as her head swirled.
And she had an idea when her thoughts finally unfurled.

She looked out her window at the hills,
The green grass, the crispy leaves and the distant windmill.
She figured she had to help the world not go downhill.

She dreamt of a world where there was no pollution,
No hunger, no recession, she needed to find a solution
To the problems in this world since evolution.

It wasn't enough to just sit there and dream,
She had to do something to make her plan go upstream
And turn this little dream into something like a joyous gleam.

But what would she do? She's just a teen.
How could she make this dream scene
Into something real, not on screen?

She had this dream, a dream so real that she forgot she was dreaming,
A dream that she found so great and appealing
And to make it come true, all she had to do was keep dreaming
Until the day she had a say and her dream could be gleaming
And her life would no more be worthless and unappealing.

Natasha Rai (14)
Barnhill Community High School, Hayes

3

The Special Moments In My Life

There have been special moments in my life
The ones that will last a lifetime through.
There have been special moments in my life,
That I will remember even at 72!
There have been special moments in my life
That will never disappear
But instead
Will constantly and emotionally reappear.
Like a shooting star in the middle of the night
I will always remember those special fights,
When my sister was as angry as a bull,
Because I had told her she wasn't very cool.
Oh even the time I had a dream
That one day I would marry a queen!
But the most important day of all
Was when I went to the civic hall.
I have had some pretty exciting days,
Which I will remember forever,
For those memories will always be
My number one treasure.

Tapiwa Mandivey (12)
Barnhill Community High School, Hayes

I Have A Dream

I have a dream that there is no war.
I have a dream that there is no terrorism.
People need more jobs, people need medicines.
Lots of people have AIDS.
I have a dream that AIDS is gone.

But it's only a dream, it may even happen.
I wish that people were not dying.
But it's only a wish, no one can do it.

Dominik Dobrenko (13)
Barnhill Community High School, Hayes

My Parents

My parents inspire me,
My parents comfort me,
My parents change my frowns,
Into big shiny smiles.
My parents.
Even though I may struggle,
My parents help with my troubles,
They both work with all their might,
All the way through day and night.
My parents.
My parents are like a light in a dark room,
My parents are my sunshine,
My parents guide my soul,
My parents are my shining star.
My parents.
My parents have kept my reputation,
So I can show the next generation.
My parents.

Yussuf Yussuf (13)
Barnhill Community High School, Hayes

My Poem

Sometimes I feel like a motherless child,
A long way from home,
Sometimes I feel like a motherless child,
I want to feel at home.

Sometimes I feel like I'm almost gone,
Like no one can see or hear me,
Sometimes I feel like I'm almost gone,
I want people to notice me.

Sometimes I feel like a feather in the air,
As I spread my wings and fly,
Sometimes I feel like a feather in the air,
I can achieve anything I want if I can fly high.

Sometimes I feel I can win,
I can gain progress if I try,
Sometimes I feel I can win,
I now know I can win as the days go by.

Deanna Spiro (13)
Barnhill Community High School, Hayes

Anything Can Happen!

If Man can walk on the moon,
Anything can happen!
If caterpillar can create a cocoon,
Anything can happen!
If Obama is president,
Anything can happen!
If life is on Mars
Anything can happen!
If quintuplets can be born,
Anything can happen!
If there were cavemen with sticks
And now women and men with cars,
Anything can happen!

Hodan Abdullahi (12)
Barnhill Community High School, Hayes

I Have A Dream

I have a dream about Jackie Chan
He's in the mighty dragon clan
He is fearsome and mighty
And he can beat off an army of fifty.

I have a dream about Jackie Chan
He's always got a better, brilliant, brave plan
There will always be this one Jackie
Don't try to be like him or you won't be so lucky.

I have a dream about Jackie Chan
Because he is the man
Give him a fight
Then feel his might.

Alexander Xu (13)
Barnhill Community High School, Hayes

7

In My Corner

In my corner
I will sit
Looking round
For that person
That warm hand
That I once knew
But then that hand went cold
And turned on me
Lack of money?
Lack of love more like
That hand that was so warm
Brought me here
Tied me up
And left me to die
I'm very cold
And very hungry
All I need is one warm hand
Again
And I will be happy
Maybe it was my fault
That that warm hand
Decided
That one day it would
Come and leave me here
I thought they would come back
And so I didn't understand
Why the hand put me down here
And left me here to die
I loved that warm hand
And it loved me
It fed me and stroked me
And then that day came
And now
I am here
I wish I was warm again
And I had a warm hand
That would feel me
And love me
And would never leave me

Here to die
I will never stop thinking
About that warm hand
That loved me
And if that warm hand will come again
I will understand
I'm not one to hold a grudge
But will be grateful
For that warm hand
Will be the hand to take me somewhere else
Here,
Is a cold place
Where no warm hand comes to love
People throw their rubbish here
Without a second thought
No one comes to visit me
It is a lonely place
And all I want
Is a kiss
Or maybe a bowl of food
I'm very hungry
And very scared
I wish that warm hand would come back
I feel myself getting weaker
Cars drive by
I try to bark
For some help
For the chance that they will hear me
But no one ever hears me
So in my corner
I will sit
Looking round
For the warm hand that I once knew.

Alice Taylor (14)
Bishop's Hatfield Girls' School, Hatfield

Pollution

You can't see the sun,
No birds,
Without trees you can't breathe.

When you walk out of your house,
When you look up to the sky,
When you can't feel the sun on your face anymore,
When you start to feel low,
It's time to change the world.

When you get in your car,
When you go to the beach,
When you can't sleep,
When you see that pollution is all around us,
It's time to change the world.

When you can't breathe in fresh air,
When you can't see the goodness of nature anymore,
When you can't use your car without feeling guilty,
When you can't change what's already happening,
It's time to change the world.

When you want your children to feel the fresh, cool breeze
                                        on their faces as they play,
When you want your children to enjoy the beauty
                                        of the natural world,
When you want your children to see the world,
When you want your children to grow up in a safe, natural place,
It's time to change the world.

When you can't see the best of nature,
When you don't want to live in a world full of pollution and mess,
When you can't see the beauty the world used to bring,
When you can see this has to end,
It's time to change the world.

Jazzmin Shapcott (14)
Bishop's Hatfield Girls' School, Hatfield

10

Inner Beauty

When you wake up in the morning,
What do you see?
Inner beauty or ugly?
It shouldn't matter what you look like,
It should be how you feel.
Try to remember the feeling,
Of being someone real.

When you walk out the door,
And you're looking all around.
You try to spot that someone,
Who looks at you and frowns.
You can't help but wonder,
What they think inside.
You can't help feeling,
Of going home to hide.

When you're sitting in your office,
And you reach for the cake.
Everyone is thinking,
What about her weight?
It's hurting deep inside you,
Should it matter if you're fat?
The world's all about looks,
And it shouldn't be like that.

Why do people judge?
It's the inside that counts,
It's not about your beauty,
Nor your money amount.
Your mother doesn't judge you,
Nor your friends and family too.
So where do the barriers come from?
Perhaps it could be you.

Georgina Cook (14)
Bishop's Hatfield Girls' School, Hatfield

Listen

She sits up in her room, thinking for a reason.
A reason why she doesn't feel the seasons.
The time just passes by.
All she does is cry.

What causes all this pain?
Why is she full of shame?
She doesn't ever feel.
Her cuts don't seem to heal.

She has no other way.
It's how she gets through every day.
She can't possibly speak out.
But she really wants to shout!

She carries on the only way she knows.
Where she is no wind will blow.
A pool of blood appears on the floor.
But she will carry on for sure!

Will they ever know?
Will her feelings ever show?
Her eyes are full of fright.
This will be her final night.

All she did was cry.
The time just passed her by.
She didn't even shout.
Oh how I wish she did speak out!

Holly Paton (14)
Bishop's Hatfield Girls' School, Hatfield

But I Am Me

I may be black,
I may be white,
I may be red,
I may be green,
I may be all the colours in-between,
But I am me . . .

I may be fat,
I may be thin,
I may be tall,
I may be short,
I may be bigger than anything you have ever thought,
But I am me . . .

I may be loud,
I may be calm,
I may be confident,
I may be shy,
Who knows, I may even be a tiny bit sly,
But I am me . . .

And you are you,
And we are we,

We are all different,
Individual,
Special!

Lorna Johnson (13)
Bishop's Hatfield Girls' School, Hatfield

Perfection

The girl across the room gives me a stare,
I look away to hide that I care,
I stumble and walk as I leave at a fast pace,
Is it my clothes, my body, my hair, my face?
I know they're looking at me, I can see it in their eyes,
Every time they look at me I know it's me that they despise,
I try to skip every meal and try to lose that weight,
People stop to stare at me because I'm seven stone eight,
My face is filled with craters, spots and wrinkles too,
No boy has even looked at me, but there is nothing I can do.
When I look in the mirror, guess what I see,
An ugly fat beast staring back at me,
The tears always roll down each cheek,
How come I'm this way, how come I'm a freak?
The meals I skip and the pills I take,
Stop me reaching for that last slice of cake,
Who cares if I faint and feel dizzy now and again?
I hate being this way; I hate being in pain,
So what if I'm weak? So what if I'm tired?
All I want is to be admired,
I know they all laugh at me and think, *what do you call that?*
It's them that make me who I am,
It's them that make me fat.

Eloise Shackleton (13)
Bishop's Hatfield Girls' School, Hatfield

Why Me?

With fear, anger, pain,
Through the school gates I walk,
Fists clenched, head down
I wander aimlessly
Hoping to be unnoticed,
Hoping to be one of them.

A shout pierces my brain,
Like a jagged piece of glass cutting me in half,
A taunt, a whisper, a nudge,
Eyes hunting me down,
They've spotted me, I am no longer invisible,
I carry on walking, desperate to escape.

The bell rings out, saving me,
Going to registration,
A welcome distraction,
I head towards my classroom,
I sit at my desk alone,
I hear a few sniggers and hurtful whispers,
I sit quietly at my desk waiting for the next bell,
Sending me back into the lions' den.

Hannah Kenworthy (14)
Bishop's Hatfield Girls' School, Hatfield

What Is Poverty?

What is poverty?
Having no food and excessive hunger is poverty,
Being homeless and having poor shelter is poverty,
Starving and having no money for food is poverty,
Having no money to buy medical supplies for your dying child is poverty,
Only having dirty and diseased water to drink and wash in is poverty,
That is poverty!

Charlotte Manners (14)
Bishop's Hatfield Girls' School, Hatfield

Our Innocent World And Us, Its People

The soft white fur of the polar bear,
The sweet smell of flowers in the air,
The deep forest of lush green colour,
The pure blue of the running river,
The quiet hum of the countryside,
The calm lullaby of the sea's tide,
The morning sun with its ruby-red glow,
The bright white of the thick mountain snow,
The joyful songs of the birds in the sky,
The rising moon as the sun says goodbye.

Why keep ourselves from such wonderful things?
Why be like nature's tyrants not human beings?
If only we cared about our suffering Earth,
If only we realised what it's really worth.
We're causing extinction and pollution,
We're destroying all of God's great creation.
Think of the difference we all could make,
Think that if we ignore, our lives we will take.
Our innocent world will soon retaliate,
Us, its people, must act before it's too late . . .

Melody Blanc (13)
Bishop's Hatfield Girls' School, Hatfield

If You're Not Yourself Then Who Are You?

Who are you?
You were one and now are two
You were perfect . . .
Now you're like everyone else.

Be yourself

You never used to wear that
Why all the sudden change?
I understand you're growing but you always used to range.

Be yourself.

Who are you out with?
Why are you being so sly?
I know you're getting older but you used to be so shy.

Be yourself

Wear your own clothes,
Do what you want,
I'm sure you'll be fine,
Just stick with your mind.

Laura Aldridge (14)
Bishop's Hatfield Girls' School, Hatfield

Life . . .

Life
It brings so many opportunities
Life
Many choices to make
Life
It's like a puzzle waiting to be solved
Life
It can be hard to live
Life . . .

Starvation
Is for the poor and unfortunate
Starvation
The amount of food has been cut
Starvation
Think of the millions waiting and waiting
Starvation
The food that sits on our plate and then goes in the bin
Starvation . . .

Talaynia Samuel & Sonia Jolly (13)
Bishop's Hatfield Girls' School, Hatfield

Waste

Seasons come and seasons go,
Pollution blocks the river's flow,
Litter blowing in the air,
No one steps, no one cares,
Chemical waste, swirling in rivers,
Poisoned voles share their last shivers,
Puffs of cigarette smoke,
Filling animals' lungs to choke,
Tin cans cutting dolphins' noses,
The blood that drips, as red as roses,
Rubbish buried under the ground,
Neither lost, neither found,
Cars wasting oil,
No nutrients for the soil,
Help your planet today,
And watch the world bloom,
In its naturally gorgeous array.

Billie Coletta (13)
Bishop's Hatfield Girls' School, Hatfield

First Love

As she saw him walk down the street,
She felt her heart skip a beat.
Knowing he would cross her way,
Brightened up her whole day.
Step by step he was getting nearer,
And suddenly his face looked clearer.
As he walked past she knew him more,
There was something about him she couldn't help but adore.
Her feelings for him were unbelievable,
A glimpse of his eyes was almost receivable.
Closer and closer the pair advanced,
She looked his way and caught a glance.

Mia Nosworthy (14)
Bishop's Hatfield Girls' School, Hatfield

A Stereotypical Poem About Stereotyping

Stereotyping has gripped the nation,
Adored by those who lack imagination.
And sadly people don't seem to care,
If they are judged purely by what they wear.

People, all totally different inside,
Behind their mask of uniformity they hide.
They've forgotten what it's like to be unique,
To them non-conformity seems lonely and bleak.

Emos, Divas, Hoodies, Boffs,
Skaters, Chavs, Jocks and Goths.
People often ask 'To which do you belong?'
But I think labelling is simply wrong.

Jasmin Evison-Jones (13)
Bishop's Hatfield Girls' School, Hatfield

Just Hungry Or Starving To Death?

World hunger, a threat to so many lives,
Worse than drugs or alcohol or knives.
Poverty, a situation that makes so many die,
While we throw away a third of the food we buy.
Starvation, a painful way to meet your end,
We watch our pets die, they watch family and friends.
If we could feel their pain, that they suffer each day,
We'd appreciate what we have in such a different way.
Give us a donation, give yourself peace of mind,
Whether big or small, be generous and kind.
Give us a donation, help if you can,
Show us you're devoted, give a helping hand.

Audrey Shulman (14)
Bishop's Hatfield Girls' School, Hatfield

The Cherry Blossom - Haikus

Sitting on a tree
Baby-pink looking pretty
Then it falls, falls, falls.

When the winter comes
The cherry blossom rains down
And spreads love to all.

When the spring comes round
The pink blossom blooms again
For us to cherish.

When the summer comes
The blossom is in full bloom
And bud has broken.

When the autumn draws
Those long, harsh, dark nights of old
The lingering calm.

How can just one thing
Something so small, so fragile
Change the entire Earth?

The beauty of such
Can inspire the hearts of men
Then, can change the world.

Sitting in a tree
Baby-pink, looking pretty
Then it falls, falls, falls.

Connor Pugh (15)
Carterton Community College, Carterton

My Magic Box

(Based on 'Magic Box' by Kit Wright)

I will put in my box . . .
The run of an antelope in a lion's hunt,
The black cat spy sitting on the wall,
The bold tiger licking her cub.

I will put in my box . . .
The bark of a dog spreading across the street,
The beauty of a horse galloping in the wind,
The slither of a slimy snake in the Sahara Desert.

I will put in my box . . .
The soar of a frog escaping the feisty jaws
                              of a hungry crocodile,
The unity of a shoal of brightly coloured fish,
The golden eagle swooping elegantly for its unfortunate prey.

My box is fashioned from the elements of fire and ice,
Protected by Merlin's enchantment spell,
Contains a piece of the sun,
Crafted by God himself.

I shall surf with the turtles in my box,
Swim with dolphins in my box,
Dive into a volcano in my box,
Then I shall sleep in my box.

Keir Campbell (11)
Carterton Community College, Carterton

Change Is Creation

Change is creation that makes all our nations,
Creation is war's dominion.
We squabble like children for petty misfortune.
We'll never forever be one.

James England (15)
Carterton Community College, Carterton

Love That Cat

Love that cat,
With his sandpaper tongue.
Love that cat,
With fur so soft.
Love that cat,
Who will keep all my secrets,
Yes it's true . . .
I love that cat.

Megan Pearson (12)
Carterton Community College, Carterton

I Have A Dream . . .

I went to sleep one night
As I was having a dream
I was driving in Nascar
It was black, red and green.

My first race was the Daytona 500
The hardest track in the world
I jumped into my car
But I couldn't see as my vision was blurred.

My first lap was at an end
Just another 200 to go
My adrenaline was rushing through me
But I was driving slow.

I put my foot down
As I really wanted to win
Soon I became first
Hopefully I wouldn't spin.

Soon the race ended
I was smiling like a fool
My mum said, 'Wake up dear boy,
You're going to be late for school.'

Ashish Patel (14)
Copland Community College, Wembley

23

I Have A Dream

I have a dream
That maybe one day
The world will be a better place.
No hate, no racism, no reason for dismay.

I want to live in a world,
Where there's no wish for others to leave it.
Suicide shouldn't be the answer
If only some could believe it.

We should be encouraged to learn and do something great
In a better, safer environment
Where we are understood not brought down,
Being different doesn't mean you deserve hate.

It's easy to stereotype and judge.
Hate the ones we know nothing about.
Fill everyone's mind with hate,
Hypocrisy and doubt.

I have a dream, that everyone should be treated fairly.
Judged by them and not by their skin.
I have a dream, where the world is a safer place.
But I only ever find this rarely.

A crippled world, bitter and violent.
Gun and knife crime, drugs and murder, who is to blame?
I have a dream.
That maybe, one day things won't be the same.

Maybe it's time for a change.
Maybe we should start trying.
Maybe we should change.
I have a dream,
That one day,
Maybe my world will be a better place.

Krishna Halai (14)
Copland Community College, Wembley

I Have A Dream

I have a dream that the world will be full of happiness,
And that everyone will respect each other
No matter what race they are.
That all countries will unite together and help each other,
That there will be no violence in the world
And everyone will live in freedom.

I have a dream that one day there will be no knife crime,
No smoking and no drugs.
That we will not have to be scared as we walk down the street,
That we will live forever
And will never have to be stressed out about anything in life.

I hope that the technology will improve
And that no one will ever get sick or hurt.
I dream that we can always stay young and never turn old,
And we will love one another like we love our brothers and sisters,
And everyone will be treated fairly.

One day I will wake up and feel the fresh air rise in my lungs
And there will be no pollution in the world
And that the world will feel like Heaven
The wealth will be fairly distributed among the rich and poor
And people will not live in poverty.
But most of all, I dream that I will end up in Heaven.

Sohaib Rahmathullah (14)
Copland Community College, Wembley

25

I Have A Dream

I have a dream that there was a safer environment,
I have a dream that one day the world would start over again.
I have a dream that everyone is treated the same,
It's only you to blame.
I have a dream that one day anyone can walk anywhere
Without being afraid of being stabbed or shot.

I have a dream that one day we will collect all weapons and burn them.
I have a dream that one day there will be no such thing
                              as racism and disrespect.
I have a dream that one day the world will change
                    into a better and safer place to live.

I have a dream that everyone will be able to have jobs
Without being worried that they will be rejected because of their colour.
I have a dream that there will be no hatred in life.
I have a dream that this world will be a non-violent place.
I have a dream that there will be no gangs.
I have a dream that there will be no smoking and drugs.

But my big dream is that one day
My dream will come true if we work together.

Bijal Mepani (13)
Copland Community College, Wembley

Dreams, Dreams, What Do They Mean?

Dreams, dreams, what do they mean?
Do they mean soaring high in the sky?
Climbing a mountain high?
Marrying your dream guy?
Or learning how to fly?
Do they mean a world full of peace?
Do they mean a world with no hatred?

Dreams, dreams, what do they mean?
Do they mean being a dancer or a doctor?
Do they mean having lots of friends?
Do they mean a life with no bullying?
Do they mean having long, curly hair?
Is it being different and not being bothered to care?

Dreams, dreams, what do they mean?
My dream is to reach the top and never stop.
My dream is to have lots of kids.
My dream is to have a grand house.
My dream is to have a great life.
That is my dream, what is yours?

Rachel Ayeh-Datey (14)
Copland Community College, Wembley

My World Dream

This poem is about equal rights throughout the world.
A wise man once said,
It doesn't matter about the colour of your skin,
But the content of your character.
Doesn't matter if you are black or white,
Just be bright,
Know that everyone has equal rights.
Put your foot down, unite as one
And put a stop to racism.

Amira Hassan (12)
Copland Community College, Wembley

I Have A Dream

I have a dream
To conquer the world
And help the poor
Stop the wars
And make the world a happier place.

I have a dream
To help justice
And kill the violence
Serve the law
And make the world a happier place.

I have a dream
To see the world
Discover planets
And be a scientist
And make the world a happier place.

I have a dream
To make the world a better place.

Fatima Zribi (12)
Copland Community College, Wembley

I Have A Dream

I have a dream
That one day the world will come to an end,
I was about to enter Heaven,
So there I was standing outside the gates of Heaven,
When I looked down I saw everything from the Earth,
Being lifted into the air and crumbling into nothing.

I have a dream that I saw others,
Going into the pits of Hell,
Shouting, screaming, begging for the pain to end,
The gates of Heaven were opening for me to enter,
I saw the light and started walking into the mist.

Salman Khan (13)
Copland Community College, Wembley

I Have A Dream

Dreams, people think that they will never be reality,
I have a dream that people of all nations will come as one,
Black and white will be treated as one.

Rumbles of earthquakes will never be heard again,
Hurricanes will no longer sweep through the land,
A cyclone will just be a breath of wind.

Eagles and mice will eat as one,
Not each other,
Lions and lambs basking in the sun.

A dream where tears of happiness will be heard everywhere,
Old one's flesh restored as in childhood,
Man and beast will live together in harmony.

Murdering and war will end,
No more suffering or illness,
Life will be a paradise.

I have a dream.

Alanya-Jessica Johnstone (12)
Copland Community College, Wembley

World Peace

I have a dream where there will be world peace
People living in a calm world.
Children playing and relaxing
Reminding us, what war has done
People! People! Listen, look around you.
Stop killing each other
Spread peace and love
Make this world a better place for our children
And our grandchildren.

Meher Deboo (11)
Copland Community College, Wembley

I Have A Dream

I have a dream that this world was free,
Free from frustration or anger.
I have this thing in my heart,
This thing is happiness and love,
Oh, I have a dream.

Oh no, this world was led astray,
With wars, with fright,
And one day peace will be restored,
Oh yes, I have this dream,
That the world was not far away.

This is reality,
Not like bad things never happened,
No black, no white, just mixed race,
That this world had no blackmail,
Not to be frightened,
Not to be scared,
Oh I have a dream.

Amal Mahamed (11)
Copland Community College, Wembley

I Have A Dream

I have a dream
That one day I will be a successful person
Getting a good job
Fulfilling my wishes.

I have a dream
To be the happiest person
Be with my family and friends
Who mean the world to me.

I have a dream
A very big dream
Which I want to fulfil
Before I die.

I will fight
Won't give up
Try to enjoy my life
My only one life.

Asha Gurung (14)
Copland Community College, Wembley

I Have A Dream!

I have a dream!
That one day I will become a famous and successful lawyer.
I have a dream!
That I will achieve great results in life.
I have a dream!
That I will be a successful lawyer
The world can trust with their cases.
I have a dream!
That I will have a great family and friends
Who back me with my dreams.
I have a dream!
I have a very big dream!

Olitiana Dervishi (14)
Copland Community College, Wembley

I Have A Dream

I have a dream . . .
That one day the Earth will come to an end,
And all the Earth's belongings will crumble like a pie.
I have a dream . . .
That the meteorite will be rocketing towards Earth
At the speed of 500 miles per hour.
I have a dream . . .
That the flaming hot meteor will crash into London,
London will bake like an apple crumble.
I have a dream . . .
That the London Eye will rot like a stinking fish,
The strings will burn and the eye will roll down the streets.

I have a dream . . .
That one day these dreams
Would come true.

Dipak Bariya (13)
Copland Community College, Wembley

We Are All The Same!

I once had a dream,
That we were all the same,
I woke up and the world,
Was a different game,
It burnt everyone,
It burnt with a strong flame,
Black or white,
They're not to blame for who they are,
We are all people,
It is my dream to be seen as equal,
Black, white, fat, slim,
It's my dream to show that,
Equality, that is my dream,
I hope it is yours too.

Hanaa Ennasr Elidrissi (13)
Copland Community College, Wembley

I Have A Dream

I have a dream,
To feed the poor,
To rule the world,
But not break the law.

I have a dream,
To see the world from the moon,
Be the first person on Mars,
But not break the law.

I have a dream,
To help others,
To save them,
But not break the law.

I have a dream
To keep the world out of trouble!

Yasmin McDonnell (11)
Copland Community College, Wembley

My Very Special Dream

I have a dream,
A very special dream,
Which will change my life,
With bright light beams,
Shining on the guy,
Who is my role model,
And will help me succeed to reach my dreams!

My dream,
A very special dream,
Will become true one day,
Then, without any stress,
I will say,
'I'm a Bollywood actress!'

Amalia Premgi (14)
Copland Community College, Wembley

Our World - What Is Happening?

Our world is changing.
It is different to what we had.
It's not all good, but it's not that bad.
All these problems need to be solved
And they can be if we all get involved.
Barack Obama became President of the United States
It was a historic day, you must remember these dates.
Wars, poverty, racism and crime - there needs to be a stop!
We cannot have this world's greatness come to a drop.
The world needs peace and harmony, no killing, no fighting.
Problems, problems, problems!
Troops in Afghanistan and the credit crunch.
Jeez, that is a big bunch!
There are so many issues that need to be solved.
But if the world acts like one, we will get it done!

Janki Amin (13)
Copland Community College, Wembley

I Have A Dream

I have a dream,
To be heard and seen.
That one day all nations will find happiness
Embracing each other
With friendship and kindness to each other's colour.

I have a dream,
That peace will replace war,
And knife and gun crime will be no more.
That racism will no longer exist,
And all people will live in happiness.

I have a dream,
That people can walk on the street
With dignity and respect,
So that they can be treated with equality.

Rohanna Hamilton (12)
Copland Community College, Wembley

I Have A Dream

I have a dream,
A dream of a brand new tomorrow,
A dream without cruelty and sorrow!
The deaths of innocent human beings,
Are they people without feelings?
They say nothing you can do can change the world,
But I had a dream,
A dream that could change the world,
Come and join me to stop this tragedy,
The gods themselves cannot deny,
That I can change this world from a lie,
I can change this world before I die.

Ali Ghouri (12)
Dormers Wells High School, Southall

The Slave Trade

I was, I am, I will always be,
A slave through and through,
One minute, one day, forever,
All alone, no help, no relief,
All time, eternity,
Will I ever be free?

I am a wealthy man,
My conscience dead,
My heart of stone,
My strings working,
My power limitless,
My orders the final word.

I am a businessman,
Who commands all,
With limitless bounds,
And money galore,
Who needs to care,
What happens below?

My life for profit,
My hand for money,
My brain for cunning over all.

I am a simple person,
With a clear conscience,
Or so I thought . . .

When you see through the web,
Of deceit and myth,
You find nothing,
But death, death and more death,
Of secret workers,
Toiling with no breaks,
Withering and dying,
No longer having any faith.

Our equals no more,
Living like the poor,
Seeing no more.

Does a man have the right to have mortal control,
Over fellow men?
Does a man have the right to silence,
The innocent?
Does a man have the right to be God?

Pascal Jones (12)
Dormers Wells High School, Southall

Violence

Day by day we are dying,
Our children are dying,
Our brothers and sisters are dying.

We are meant to be for each other,
For each other we are meant to be.
From one corner of the country, to another,
All that is in sight is bloodshed, tears, pain and grief.

A child is stabbed, the mother cries,
Not knowing what to say.
She is speechless and completely shocked,
Her baby has passed away.

Come together my friends,
We are like family, one great nation.
Be brave, stand up,
Let's all stop violence.

I have a dream, I have a dream,
Work together and stop violence.

Maryam Naz (13)
Dormers Wells High School, Southall

37

Is This Fair?

Children get bullied every day,
But who can do anything about it?
Sometimes even those who you think will help,
Walk past like it's a daily ritual.

People and campaigns say 'stop bullying',
But does the bully care?
A few pounds and credits is all he gets,
But a bruised arm and broken leg is not fair.

School is a time for fun and honesty,
A time to learn and socialise,
But for those who it turns out to be misery and despair,
To sit back and watch is truly unfair.
What is the point of stepping outside?
Knowing your life is next.
Knowing you are being spied on for every move you make next.
Is this fair?

Why should the way you look and dress,
Imply who you really are?
Don't judge a book by its cover,
What goes around comes around.
Discrimination is unfair.

Sometimes you need to view issues from both angles
                                    before you point the finger,
A bully will bully because of their past,
So empathise before you sympathise,
It's the only way it's fair.

You might not care about bullying now,
But if we don't help stop it,
You'll never know what your children will have to go through, will you?
It won't be fair for them either.

Bullying,
Is defined as just a word,
But it's much more,
It's a chapter in your life which could change you forever.
Now is this fair?

Hayat Mohamed (12)
Dormers Wells High School, Southall

I Hate War

This little word, with its big effect,
I can smell death in it,
I can see destruction within it,
It makes me feel angry,
It makes me feel sick . . . I hate war!

Why does war exist?
Why does it take innocent lives away?
Why does it take peace and happiness away?
Why do little children have to suffer because of it?
Why should it leave pain everywhere? . . . I hate war!

Is it for money?
Is it for power?
Is it just for land?
Whatever is the cause . . . I hate war!

War should be stopped,
War should be banned,
I wish it had never existed in this world . . . I hate war!

Fadel Shamel (13)
Dormers Wells High School, Southall

I Have A Dream

I have a dream
That people will stop
Killing animals.

I have a dream
That people will
Get better soon.

I have a dream
That people will
Stop smoking.

I have a dream
That people will
Stop fighting in the war.

Sam Emmett (14)
Fitzwaryn School, Wantage

I Have A Dream

I have a dream
To stop people in Africa drinking dirty water,
I have a dream
That people will stop getting ill,
I have a dream
To stop the wars,
I have a dream
To stop people taking bad drugs,
I have a dream
To stop animals being endangered,
I have a dream
To help save the world.

Chantell Louise Moffett
Fitzwaryn School, Wantage

I Have A Dream

I have a dream
No animals are in danger.
I have a dream
Make peace in the war.
I have a dream
No crime in the world.
I have a dream
Stop taking drugs in the world.
I have a dream
No murder in the world.

Brett Hemingway (13)
Fitzwaryn School, Wantage

I Have A Dream

I have a dream that smoking will cease.
I have a dream of scoring a goal for AC Milan.
I have a dream that I can play the guitar.
I have a dream where everyone is at peace.
I have a dream that I have a big house
With a wife and family.

William George Moffett (13)
Fitzwaryn School, Wantage

I Have A Dream

I have a dream about clean air
I have a dream about sailing the high seas
I have a dream of a big red boat
I have a dream of coming home safe at night.

Charles Russell (14)
Fitzwaryn School, Wantage

Happiness Is Funny

Happiness
Happiness is all around
We all need to be happy
Do we need an iPod to be happy?
Do we need lots of cool stuff to be happy?
My family makes my life more and happier.
My friends make me happy,
But some people don't know how to smile or be happy.
How can we make all this work?
Share love and happiness
Smile. Smile once in a while
Everyone should smile and be happy
Every day I think how I can make my family's faces
                                    light up with happiness
I dream the world will be happy like me.

Abbie Maple (15)
Gosden House Special School, Bramley

Everybody

Everybody is not the same
We have hearts, we have a body
But we do not have the
Same ways
Some are nice
Some are bad
Some are fat and some are slim
Some are cold and
Some are kind
But we all need to have respect
We are what we are
Everyone is different in their own way
But we all need love.

Mandy Bicknell (14)
Gosden House Special School, Bramley

If Only

If only we were kind to each other,
Nobody would get hurt.
If only we helped the children across the world,
They would be in safe arms, not in the wrong hands.
If only there was no war,
People wouldn't have to risk their lives for their country.
If only people in Africa had more food,
They wouldn't have to starve or die.
If only the world was a better place,
Everyone would have a better life.
If only this dream of mine was true.

Frankie Gale (13)
Gosden House Special School, Bramley

My Dream

My world would be nice
I dream of going to Dubai
I really want to go there.
I dream of living with my sister
She is always there for me.
I dream of getting me a car
It will be so cool.
I dream of being able to eat like everybody else.
I dream of not going to hospital all the time.
I have had so many operations.

Sanna Iqbal (15)
Gosden House Special School, Bramley

I Have A Dream

If I could I would
Sprinkle magic dust on bad people to make them good
Stop people fighting and make them friends
Find a cure to make sick people better
Have enough food so that no one is hungry
Make sure that everyone has a place to live and a school to learn.
This is my dream.

Laura Metcalfe (15)
Gosden House Special School, Bramley

Racism Wrong

Racism
Racism
Racism
Stop, stop the racism
It hurts people's feelings
It affects people's lives

Keep the peace and don't hate
It's only a colour, it's just a race,
It affects you if it doesn't affect them
Keep the peace and don't hate

Put yourself in their shoes
How would you feel?
What would you do?
Would you like to be discriminated against?
And called every name under the sun?
How would you feel?
What would you do?
Keep the peace
Keep the peace
Don't hate, love
Don't hate, love.

Alisha Abbey & Darrell Manning
Hazeley School, Milton Keynes

Drug Muck

Like a candle,
Small and thin,
Smooth and fragile,
With good stuff within.

You light up,
It makes the world look great
You breathe it in
The world turns to hate.

In your mouth with
Every breath and every smoke
It makes the ugly guys
Look like fit blokes.

You try one,
Then want another,
Show your friends,
Show your brother.

Now you're in,
The smoky pit,
You've had your fun
Now you'll have your fits.

Welcome to the world
Of blackened doom,
Of your memory,
Stuck in gloom.

Once you're in
Can't get out,
No more fun,
That is all out.

Don't try it,
Or you'll be stuck
In the pit of hurt
The *drug* muck.

Heidi Sweet (14)
Hazeley School, Milton Keynes

Poverty!

Poverty
You don't know what it feels like

Imagine
Going even one day without food

Death
Dying because you don't have enough money

Children
Not being able to go to school and learn anything

Pain
Sadness, sickness, suffering

Poverty
You can help!

Imagine
People looking at you and thinking you are ugly

Friends
Having no friends or family to love you

Torture
Some thinking they are bigger than you
And abusing you

Jobs
Being unemployed
Because you couldn't go to school

Are you just going to sit there
And let this happen?

Stop poverty!
Give money!
Help people!

Courtnae Butcher (14)
Hazeley School, Milton Keynes

Tomorrow

Tomorrow
Is the air clean?
Tomorrow
Are trees still standing?
Tomorrow
Are the fields green?
Tomorrow
Are apples on the trees?
Tomorrow
Are there still rainforests?
Tomorrow
Are there still ice caps?
Tomorrow
Are tigers in zoos?
Tomorrow
How many animals are left?
Tomorrow
Are fish in the sea?
Tomorrow
Is the water drinkable?
Tomorrow
What's left that's not manmade?
Tomorrow
Is the Earth still standing?
Tomorrow
Will we change?

Thomas Laing (14)
Hazeley School, Milton Keynes

The Silent War

No guns
No knives
No bombs
No war.

Guns kill
Knives kill
Bombs kill
War kills.

Standing at gunpoint
Standing at knifepoint
Standing at bombpoint
Standing in war.

Running from guns
Running from knives
Running from bombs
Running from war.

Living with guns
Living with knives
Living with bombs
Living with war.

Today it's them
Tomorrow it could be you
So, what will you do?

Ryan Nolan & Aaron Rawlinson (13)
Hazeley School, Milton Keynes

The Nightmare

I have a nightmare,
When I look around,
Of what people have created,
Black people getting bullied,
My nightmare is real!

I have a nightmare,
When I look around,
All the hate and the war,
All the screaming sounds,
Between black and white,
My nightmare is real!

I have a nightmare,
It's a turf war on a global scale,
I am tired of hatred,
I am tired of this devil,
I am tired of this stuff
Happening over and over again,
My nightmare is real!

My nightmare is stopped,
No more racism,
No more killing.
A miracle has happened today,
Hooray!

James Rioch & James Stainsby (13)
Hazeley School, Milton Keynes

Nameless

I could have a dream, or I could part the Red Sea.
But all of this would make you think of me.
But I don't want your pity; I don't want your fame.
I don't even want you to remember my name.
I'm not important; at least not to you.

Nathan Burnikell (14)
Hazeley School, Milton Keynes

49

Stand Up

Just stop and think!
If there was a world with no war.
Nobody killing
Nobody dying.
Nobody crying.
Innocent children smiling also laughing.
If there was a world with no war.
Imagine the joy it would bring.
Imagine the happiness it would bring.
Be brave.
Be bold.
Stand up to war.
Stand up for peace.
Stand up for love not hate.
Stand up for those children crying.
Stand up for those children dying.
Just stop and think of the people dying.
The people crying.
The people hurting.
While you're eating and sleeping.
They have nothing
Do the right thing
Say no to war!

Akosua Darko (13)
Hazeley School, Milton Keynes

Give People Jobs - George Bush

I think that people should be given jobs
Because they could become homeless.
They'll become homeless
And won't have anything to eat.
Also, just to eat
They will most likely nick things from shops.

Rhys Barrett
Hazeley School, Milton Keynes

Stand Out, Speak Out

In our modern world we still see racism.
Racism for what we believe in and where we are from.
If God, whichever god you believe in,
Intended us to all look the same,
Why are we different?
Stand out, speak out for what you believe in,
Make your voice stand out, don't shy away.

If God intended us to be racist,
What kind of world do we live in?
No one likes to be treated differently because of their skin.
We have our own mind and believe in what we want to believe in.
We are individual and that's what makes us beautiful,
Why are we fooled into thinking
We have to look a certain way and be perfect?
Would you like your children to think like this?

Have you ever thought that someone was going to be less
Because they are from a different country?
Open your minds, free your soul,
And we could create a better world!

Saiorse Collins (14)
Hazeley School, Milton Keynes

Stop War

W ill this ever stop?
O r is this just going to carry on?
R unning out of troops as we move closer
L and being lost to the enemy
D ays go by

W orld war is not being stopped
A ction, bombs, guns, deaths
R ed blood, lots of red blood.

Lewis Strong (11)
Hazeley School, Milton Keynes

51

Imagine

Imagine
If you got bullied because of your skin colour.
Imagine
If you had to go days and days without food.
Imagine
If your dream can't come true because of the colour of your skin.
Imagine
If you cannot afford a house and are forced to live on the streets.
Imagine
Not being able to go to the school of your dreams because of your race.
Imagine
Being jobless because of your race.
Imagine
If you got attacked because of your race.
Imagine
Not being able to marry the person you love because of your race.
Imagine
A world without racism.
Imagine
Tomorrow!

Kauthar Abdulrasheed (14)
Hazeley School, Milton Keynes

The World

I had a dream that one day the world would be safe.
No graffiti, bullies, lakes of grime and tramps with a sad face.
First we will talk about graffiti on the walls
And then the tramps of the streets
The graffiti destroys our world
Painting art where the police just swirled
And they do it again.
Act soon or you will be in a right mess!

Mitchell Schofield
Hazeley School, Milton Keynes

Footballer

You start as a kid
You kick about and play
And if you keep trying, trials will come your way
And if you do well they may sign you on
And from then on your career has begun.
A few years later and you're still getting better
The manager's happy and he writes you a letter
Your debut comes the next Saturday
A last-minute winner and the fans are chanting your name.
The next week you go and do it again
The fans go mental and cheer again.
A month later you're still playing great
Chelsea come in and show you their gate.
The next day you're on the front page
Signing a shirt which on the back has your name.
You make a big impact and score loads of goals
You grow old and support in the cold
You finally die and the fans stand in silence
For a legend who scored and made them champions.

Ben Head (14)
Hazeley School, Milton Keynes

I Don't Want Daddy

The bruises spread every Saturday night,
The scars grow and so does the fright.
The anger builds up after every drink,
The yelling starts, it hurts to blink.
I scream,
I curse,
I worry,
I hurt,
I cry,
I don't want Daddy to make me die!

Stephanie O'Dell (13)
Hazeley School, Milton Keynes

Litterbug

Bushes full of crisp packets,
Pick it up,
Pavements caked in beer cans,
Pick it up,
Plastic bags hanging off trees,
Pick it up,
Plastic bags scattered in ditches,
Pick it up,
Syringes paving skateboard parks,
Pick it up,
McDonald's packets flying across roads,
Pick it up,
Cigarettes stuck on curbs,
Pick it up,
Spray paint cans in underpasses,
Pick it up,
Is this what you want your kids' world to look like?
If no, pick it up!

Matt Williamson (13)
Hazeley School, Milton Keynes

Make The World A Better Place

I have a dream that the war against Palestine and Israel will stop
I have a dream that all people spoiling every religion's name will stop
It is putting us against each other.

I have a dream that we will not be disgraced
We are what we are
The world is not free from danger
Let's put our hands together and let peace rise
So we will all enjoy our time that we have left
Make ourselves proud and let ourselves out
And make ourselves proud.

Farida Hussaini (12)
Hazeley School, Milton Keynes

The Beauty In Life

Even though you're not near,
Life goes on while I shed a tear,
There are so many beautiful things in life
Some things that can be ripped with a knife
Don't worry about all your sorrow
There's always another day like tomorrow.

So why waste another breath talking
When you could be outside right now walking?
There are so many beautiful things to see
Like freedom and nature such as a bee
The seasons are so lovely like you and me
I'm sure you'll agree it's like a cup of tea.

Go and enjoy the beauty of life
While you can, with your mother or wife
Remember, life's beauty is hard to see
But if you're clever you will live wonderfully.

Klaudia Lawman (13)
Hazeley School, Milton Keynes

Everyone Is Special In Their Own Way

Whether you're black, white or mixed race,
Or in society differently placed,
Keep in mind every day,
That everyone is special in their own way.

Wherever in the world you are from,
In whatever shape, colour or form,
Wherever now that you may stay,
Remember everyone is special in their own way.

Never believe for a second
Into disaster you are beckoned,
As a doctor, father or mother become you may,
Always remember everyone is special in their own way.

Tugse Gazioglu (14)
Hazeley School, Milton Keynes

Cruelty To Animals

C ruel is wrong
R espect your animals
U nderstand their feelings
E ntertain and play with them
L ove and attention
T ogether with your pet
Y ou look after them

T alk to them
O wn your animals

A nimals are living things
N ature with their habitat
I nterest with looking after them
M ates with your pet
A nimals at home
L ovely to see them live
S pecial thing ever.

Eleni
Hazeley School, Milton Keynes

Stop Racism

Racism, racism is not good
But we can work together to make it better
Stop all the bad words
Stop all the shame
Then no one would
Get blamed.
Give them respect
And then you will
Get it back.
Now that we
Are friends, let's
Call it the end.

Daniel Prescott
Hazeley School, Milton Keynes

Bullying

Bullying is harsh
You should never do it
Stop bullying now

Bullies are weak people
Who have nothing better to do
Stop bullying now

It makes people cry
They don't tell anyone
Stop bullying now

How shall we stop it?
Put an end to this madness
Stop bullying now

See something, say something
Has it happened to you yet?
Tell someone now please.

Ella Higgins & Eloise Kerr (13)
Hazeley School, Milton Keynes

Stop Racism

There is no difference between black and white
We are all the same
We are all human
So what's the point?
All it is, is different skin tones.
All it does is hurt people
But it should not be happening
Because we are all the same
If you do not do it
You cannot take the blame
It is not fair, it is not right
Because what is the difference
Between black and white?

Honor Jenkins (12)
Hazeley School, Milton Keynes

57

Stop War Today!

Imagine a world of hurt and pain,
Of women and children imprisoned by chains.
Imagine a world of sorrow and famine,
Of doors of lives always slamming.
Imagine a world of guns and knives,
Of countries built on bogus lies.

This is the world in which we live.

Imagine a world of joy and laughter,
Of the smiles that we are always after.
Imagine a world of wonder and love,
Of the sun shining brightly from up above.
Imagine a world of food and learning,
Of these things, we are always yearning.

This world could be yours tomorrow.
Stop war today.

Robyn Taylor & Chloë Wolverson-Ross
Hazeley School, Milton Keynes

Global Warming

G ive people a better life
L ook out for the world
O bserve what you recycle
B uy organic or recycled things
A ll of us can help
L ive to help the environment

W herever you are you can recycle
A nd our world matters, so look after it
R ecycle to save the polar bears
M orning to night you can recycle
I, we, you, us, can help to recycle
N ever let the polar bears die
G o on your bike, it will help to stop global warming.

Daniella Meakins (12)
Hazeley School, Milton Keynes

What Can We Do?

We can stop bullying
To help children
We can look for
Children before going
We can recycle
To help the environment
We can stop graffiti
To make the environment better
We can pick up litter
To stop pollution
We can switch off things
Not put on standby
To help electricity
So make a change now
And help this world
Be a better place.

Danica Aitken (11)
Hazeley School, Milton Keynes

Environment Acrostic

E nvironment has to change
N ow we make the world a wonderful place
V ery soon we will be too late
I cebergs are melting because of our actions
R ecycling is not an option
O xygen is running out
N ever will we die
M agnificent world will never back down
E lectricity is being wasted
N ever, ever give up
T ree seeds have to be planted.

Max Caswell
Hazeley School, Milton Keynes

59

We Must Think About . . .

We must start to think about our actions,
The environment is being ruined by us!
To stop wasting electricity
We must switch things off when not needed.

We must start to think about our transport,
We are polluting our environment by using petrol to run vehicles,
We must try to use a way of transport
Without needing petrol to run it.
For instance, we could walk or cycle to areas.

We must think about our waste,
We must try to recycle more
Or use more reusable materials.

Tasmin Kelly (11)
Hazeley School, Milton Keynes

Bullying

Stop bullying for it is bad,
It hurts you and makes you sad,
It's nasty and disgraceful,
The bullies beat you with a baseball bat.
You get pushed and shoved
And kicked as well
Sooner or later you start to swell.
And if you keep making them cry,
The people you hurt will want to die.
But if you're a bully and want to stop it,
You'll have to be a better hobbit.

Daniel Mohan (12)
Hazeley School, Milton Keynes

Hunters Are Always Hunted

I wonder why,
I wonder why, why people kill?
Some say it's for freedom.
Or sometimes for the thrill.
I just don't get hunting.
It seems pointless to me.
What we need is peace.
But some disagree.
And they throw it in the bin.
I guess I'll never win.

Ben Johnson (13)
Hazeley School, Milton Keynes

Against All Odds

A lonely wandering camel
Crossing the great dunes
Facing all adversities
In the pursuit of life
Meeting trials head on
And overcoming them
Surviving
Against all odds.

Salem Nizami (13)
Hazeley School, Milton Keynes

Graffiti

Why not do art somewhere else?
What makes you damage the environment?
Nothing is stopping you from doing art in different ways.
If you do that, the world can be a lovely place to be
And people won't be annoyed.

Sophie Vaughan
Hazeley School, Milton Keynes

Stopping The War

Stop people going out in the first place
Truce, put all of the guns down now
Open your door and say hi to your brother
Who has been fighting in the war
Point the soldiers back home
Now stop the war
Going back home
Is the best thing for a soldier.

Daniel Williams
Hazeley School, Milton Keynes

Free

Free to be whatever you want
To say anything you need to say.
Don't hold back!
Always have your opinion voiced,
Your opinion does count no matter what!
Never be told what to do.
Freedom,
It's in your hands now!

Kathrynn Cook (14)
Hazeley School, Milton Keynes

Helping The Earth

R ecycle because it's cool
E veryone pick up litter
C ycle, don't drive
Y ellow is the hot sun
C ars are not good for the environment
L ittle animals are dying
E verybody should do this.

George Bevan
Hazeley School, Milton Keynes

Recycle Acrostic

R emember to recycle all plastics
E veryone needs to recycle
C onfidence can save the world
Y ou, me, I and we can help recycle
C ount me in, I'll recycle
L ittering is bad
E verywhere you go, look out for litter.

Elysia Sykes (12)
Hazeley School, Milton Keynes

Martin Luther King

Racism surrounded the world
Racist comments were constantly heard
But one man saw the light
He changed the world for right
Martin Luther King battled the world
And came out victorious
If you ask me, the man is notorious.

Alex Ashman (11)
Hazeley School, Milton Keynes

How To Change The World

Recycle and it will make new things.
Stop racism and become friends with others.
Stop bullying and be nice to each other.
Stop graffiti and make our world look lovely.
If you do all that then the world will be a happy place
And waking up in the morning just knowing you helped.

Rebekah Harris
Hazeley School, Milton Keynes

63

Racism Acrostic

R acism hurts people
A ll together we can stop it!
C hange the world
 I f we can stop it we will live together
S top racism
M ay we live in peace.

Kelsey Williams
Hazeley School, Milton Keynes

I Wish

I wish people would stop smoking,
I wish people would stop war.
Some people are stupid
Killing our planet, our people, our lives.

I wish people would help the environment,
I wish people would stop drugs.
Some people are stupid,
Killing mankind and themselves.

I wish people would stop everything bad,
I wish people would learn about God.
And the way he spoke to Jesus.
Some people are stupid.

I wish people would go to school,
I wish people would love my family and friends,
Like the way I love you,
Some people are stupid, don't ask me why.

I wish people would do something good in their life,
I wish people would make me laugh like clowns do.
Some people just waste their life on drugs and alcohol.
Some people are stupid, don't ask me why.

Thomas Savage (12)
Highcrest Community School, High Wycombe

I Had A Dream

I had a dream about,
Appalling conditions of humanity in the war zone,
Militaries vying for the sake of the land,
Women and children hiding,
Watching poignant spectacles of sweltering infernos,
Whirlwinds of tanks shaking the foundations.

A hundred years later,
Poisonous air and land because of nuclear emission,
Bare land with no hope of life,
Skeletons walking with incurable diseases,
In the valley of despair.

I have a dream,
To halt utter destruction,
The hatred between beliefs, religions and boundaries,
And create an oasis of peace in this troubled world.

I have a dream of fierce urgency,
For the solid rock of brotherhood,
To rise from the darkness of war,
And walk through the sunlit path of peace.

Now is the time to end this brutal fighting,
And let peace sing from,
The snow blanket of Canada,
The Himalayan peaks,
The meanders of Ob,
The ding-dong of Big Ben,
And last but not least,
Let peace sing from inside our hearts,
Peace at last! Peace at last!

I have a dream today,
With faith, a dream coming true one day.

Anshuli Kumar (12)
Highcrest Community School, High Wycombe

Peace

I hope the near future will be different
No wars and mass murders
Prisons empty, only a memory of dark sins
Racial discrimination's an extinct language
And resources used sparingly
Renewable energy should dominate manmade objects
Criminal activities will hopefully halt in its menacing tracks
Wars will hopefully and soon become poor history
No nuclear bomb to settle differences
Or weapons to start wars and killings
Mankind should attempt to survive
Not slaughter itself with warfare and hatred

Why do we do this?
Kill others for saying or doing something against someone else's opinion?
For fame, glory as a criminal
Why are wars waged?
Nothing is achieved
But killing, murder and depression
Peace an impossible goal -
Or a future reality?

Kieren James Bannister (12)
Highcrest Community School, High Wycombe

Stop War

S top so no one else dies.
T oo many people are fighting, they might die.
O f all crimes, war is the most pointless.
P residents don't do anything to stop war.

W ar is pointless, why can't we be united?
A ll weapons used in war can kill innocent people.
R emember, please stop war!

James Gordon (12)
Highcrest Community School, High Wycombe

I Imagine!

I imagine a better place to live,
We want better,
We can live better,
We can be proud of the world we live in,
So many people are lazy,
Just throwing rubbish on the floor,
It's like saying,
If you have a car but don't drive it,
If you have a bike but don't ride it,
It's the same thing,
If we all have bins why don't we use them?
That's the question I want answered,
We're destroying the world,
We're destroying ourselves,
I have one word for everybody,
Stop! It's the right thing to do,
Stop littering!
We want to make the world a cleaner
Healthier environment for all to live in,
Let's look up to what we deserve,
And make the world a better place!

Olivia Noble (12)
Highcrest Community School, High Wycombe

The Graffiti Song

I walk down a road,
A road, where nobody goes,
Writings, drawings, anything you can think of,
This is graffiti.

Thinking of nothing; nothing at all,
People speaking their mind,
Leaving their mark
On the wall; the wall they artfully signed.

Reece Quincey (12)
Highcrest Community School, High Wycombe

67

Stabbed

I couldn't understand
I threw a punch but it did not land.
Now the wound is getting bigger,
The blade is still protruding,
A pain inflicted by youths so deluded.
Morally weak, mentally stupid,
They ran off shouting,
'Next time blood, you get shot!'
Now walking less and less steadily,
Praying that I see my mum's eyes once more
Then I die readily . . .

These two teenagers between them had a small knife,
By calling the police I saved a life.
I was much smarter this time,
Only because I dialled 999.

Just think about the people that have died,
And their parents mortified . . .

Keith Chikaviro (12)
Highcrest Community School, High Wycombe

Your Life - Your Way

Kill.
Prison.
Death row.
Lethal injection.
Dead.

This is the life of a killer.
Do you want yours to be the same?
Don't carry a knife or gun;
Only you will be to blame.

Hayley Costanzo (12)
Highcrest Community School, High Wycombe

Child Abuse Must Stop!

I have a dream that we stop abuse,
My dream is that we cut it loose.
It should be stopped, it's very wrong,
Come on everyone, this can't go on.

Their childhood's snatched away from them,
By extremely cruel women and men
They're beaten, starved and left to die,
The question everyone asks is, why?

What did they do to deserve all this?
They are only defenceless little kids.
What did they ever do to you?
What gives you the right to do what you do?

You can't keep them away forever,
We're reaching the very end of our tether.
A slap here, a punch there,
Bruises found everywhere.

Jay Brown (12)
Highcrest Community School, High Wycombe

Child Abuse

Child abuse is not good.
Parents do it because they think that children don't have feelings.
Some parents beat their children for the fun of it.
Most parents shouldn't be allowed kids.
When kids are being beaten sometimes they don't understand why.
Some poor child could lose his life.
In need of help but can't find it.
Just call 0800 1111 for your chance to save someone's life.
If you want to stop child abuse
Then tell someone about it.

Chantelle Meech (11)
Highcrest Community School, High Wycombe

69

I Wish

I wish for a free world,
Where plants can grow with no disturbance,
I wish for peace throughout countries,
No fights, no wars, no discrimination.

I wish that children could grow up,
The way we all did - peacefully, quietly,
When I look outside the window I should feel happy,
Not the bitter feeling I have.

How is it too hard to look after the Earth?
Treat it the way we do ourselves?
For someday the time will come when,
I'll look out the window and see nothing . . .
Nothing at all.

I wish for a free world,
Is it too much and too hard for me to ask?

Daniel Rooney (12)
Highcrest Community School, High Wycombe

Smoking, Smoking

Smoking, smoking can badly affect your health.
Smoking, smoking can badly affect your wealth.
Smoking, smoking covers your lungs in thick, black tar.
Smoking, smoking people do it in a bar.

Smoking, smoking people do it at any age.
Smoking, smoking people say it calms your rage.
Smoking, smoking makes your clothes smell bad.
Smoking, smoking makes people around you feel sad.

Stop smoking, smoking, throw your cigarettes away.
Stop smoking, smoking and you will have a better day.
Stop, smoking, smoking and you will become more healthy.
Stop smoking, smoking and you will become more wealthy.

Lauren Keen (12)
Highcrest Community School, High Wycombe

World Suffering

In a world with wars, starvation and poverty
There is dying, suffering and pain,
Needless, horrific suffering.
Why, why, why?
Needless suffering.
People eat food out of bins,
Why, why, why?
People living on the dirty, cold, wet street
Why, why, why?
Why do people needlessly die because of wars?
Why, why, why?
What did they ever do to anybody?
The world is amazing, so stop the pain:
Or what is life?

Mark Burnard (12)
Highcrest Community School, High Wycombe

Be Grateful

In a world where we stuff our face,
We forget the people in the other place,
The place where people have nothing to eat,
Nor have any shoes to cover their feet,
When we complain there's nothing on TV,
We forget some people can hardly see,
When your day is spoiled by rain,
Their day would be even more a drain,
When your video game is broken,
People don't care what they have spoken,
Do they like the world they live in?
Cause I think not to care is sin.
Anyone who's suffered in the past,
Should no more face this eternal blast.

Jack Nash (12)
Highcrest Community School, High Wycombe

If I Had It My Way

If I had it my way,
The playground would be a safer place.
If I had it my way,
Children wouldn't be bullied because of their race.
If I had it my way,
Youngsters wouldn't have to suffer.
If I had it my way,
There would be no tender or tougher.
If I had it my way,
Friendships would mend.
If I had it my way,
Bullying would end.

Tayla Williams (11)
Highcrest Community School, High Wycombe

I Have A Dream!

I have a dream that . . .
Children can be free, away from knives and guns.
Everyone can be fed and have their own homes.
I have a dream that . . .
We can all live in a safer world.
Therefore we can start to build a safer society.

Lauren Martin (12)
Highcrest Community School, High Wycombe

Cries Of The People

People dream of peace,
People dream of love,
We cry out to the entire world,
And up to the heavens above.

'Please stop fighting,
Killing and abusing,
We are destroying the world,
And it's not amusing!'

Racism, murder,
Is going further and further,
Children dream of a happy world,
Not one of violence and one of death.

Think of babies and children,
Do you want their lives to be destroyed by war?
No?
Then say, 'No more!'

Another issue that is bad,
Is that of global warming,
We have to stop it right now,
Before the world starts transforming.

This is my final plea,
My final nag,
Please stop all of these things now,
Just stop and listen once in a while,
And you will hear the cries of the people.

Iona McMillan (12)
Millais School, Horsham

I Have A Dream

I have a dream that one day we will all be equal,
Motivation will not be needed
And complete destruction on innocent people would
be out of the question.
I have a dream that someday countries will be able
to join hands with their once was enemies
and people would last a lifetime without killings and murders.
Battles would soon end up in our history.

Today I dream of no more war,
Rifles and battle guns would be demolished,
Burned at their deathly stake.
Once again countries would reunite and celebrate
The once more friendship of unity.
They would realise that jealousy is not a reason to fight or to kill.

Dream do I of pleasure in this world,
Peace for mankind and reassurance returned to our hearts.
There needs to be no more cautions of a home that is not your own,
Because everyone will be on your side.
Fear will not be needed for no one is against you.

Our world will not be split in two,
Sides arguing, disagreeing and fighting out of spite.
Do not only fear for yourselves,
Fear for your grandchildren.
Will they live through this or will World War Three
Finally happen and destroy our lives for the final time?

When our hero comes, will we save our world,
Our planet from all the horrors in the world
Which someone will have to face.
And that someone may be you.
I have a dream that when wars are over, battles have been won
And victory has been celebrated,

We will not cower or hide in our shells like turtles.
We will put an end to this, with the power of words.
War will be over!
I have a dream today.

Emily Morris (11)
Millais School, Horsham

Imagine A World

Imagine a world,
Where people were separated,
Imagine a world,
Where you could only be friends,
With some people,
Imagine a world,
Where some were slaves,
Like shadows in the night.
Imagine a world,
Which wouldn't change,
Imagine a world,
Where one man stood up,
And said:
'I want change'
Imagine a world,
Where people didn't listen,
Imagine a world,
Like that, for 27 years.
Imagine the thoughts running through his head,
Imagine the joy when he was released,
From the dark, dark hole,
And now there's a world,
Of joy and friendship,
And no more slavery,
Only friendship and joy,
And few can say:
'I helped change the world'
Words to change the world.

Oliver Davies (12)
Rodborough Technology College, Godalming

What I Want To Be

I often dream,
What I want to be,
Rich and famous,
But also happy

Do I want to be a soldier?
Definitely not,
There is way too much running,
And Afghanistan is hot

Do I want to be a dustbin man?
Wait, just let me think,
No, taking people's rubbish,
And the dustbins really stink

Do I want to be a sailor
Sailing the world's great seas,
With thunderstorms and massive waves?
Give me a land job, please!

Do I want to be a teacher?
No, that's too much work,
Looking after all the kids,
Although the holiday's a perk

Do I want to be prime minister?
Maybe for a day,
But then it would get too stressful,
At least it gets good pay!

Do I want to be a doctor
With all the guts and gore?
It may get lots and lots of respect,
And it won't be a bore . . .

Making animals well,
A vet I'd like to be,
As long as I had an assistant,
To clean up the poo and wee!

There are too many jobs around the world,
For me to decide just yet,
In a few more years,
A different answer you may get . . .

Samuel Waterfall (12)
Rodborough Technology College, Godalming

I Had A Dream

I have a dream,
That people can live in peace.
Leave behind the anger of yesterday.

No more toil which would spoil the friendship we have made.

Never again do I wish to see the wars which destroy families.
The wars which rip friendship in half.
The wars which ruin love and stamp it to the ground.

Too bad my dream was ripped up right in front of me.
The toil in the Gaza Strip,
Loads of innocent deaths you see.

Never again shall the friendship of yesterday be made up and all
forgotten of war.
Never will that happen.
Never will that be.

Too bad there is no ceasefire.
Too bad there is no freedom.

From this horrible,
Disgusting, sick and wrong thing, nobody has prevailed.

Nothing will come of this.
No one will be free.

I had a dream.
But it's been ripped in half right in front of me.
I had a dream . . .

Chris Peppitt (14)
Rodborough Technology College, Godalming

The Epsom Derby

(In memory of Emily Davison, Suffragette)

I've got to do it, got to do it.
But what about those hooves pummelling against the dry ground?
Just do it, just do it.
Thud! Thud! Thud!
I must do it, if not for myself then for the other Suffragettes.
But I'm so scared.
For women everywhere.

Don't back out now, not when you're so close to victory.
Close to death more like.
Just do it. Do it now. While you have a chance.
They're all depending on you.
Quickly just run.
But . . .
Just do it.

Here he comes, the king's horse, Anmer.
Hooves leaving a cloud of dust behind,
As they crush the few weeds brave enough to grow.
Here he comes, round the corner,
Too fast to stop.
Gasps rush through the crowd like the wind in the trees as I run
                                                    onto the track.

It's strange what you notice in your last seconds.
There's a little girl in the crowd,
Next to her father,
She has a blue ribbon in her hair,
And she is looking at me
A strange expression of confusion that suddenly flashes from
                                                    realisation to fear

There's still time to go back, still time to live.
No!
A scream and then blackness.

Did it work?

Megan Pattison (12)
Rodborough Technology College, Godalming

78

If The World Were Perfect

If the world were perfect
Evil would heal old wounds with the good

And I have a dream
Individuals would unite to make a difference for the better

If the world were perfect
Black and white would make the pieces of the checkerboard

And I have a dream
That a feeling of happiness would be a routine for the globe

If the world were perfect
The sharpest of swords will not defeat what we believe

And I have a dream
That tears of hope turn into tears of joy

If the world were perfect
Appearance would be the shadow and character the shining sun

And I have a dream
The inspiration turns all the bad into good like a life changing cycle

If the world were perfect
The tortoise would defeat the hare to the finish line

And I have a dream
That a cry for help can always be assisted

Like a deer at dusk, it can never been seen
It's a silhouette in the dark of the moonlight
A person out there never noticed
But never lets their guard down
In fighting for what they most believe
To make the world a happier place
Like Jesus nailed to the wood made cross
Sacrificed everything for their fellow peers . . .

To make my dream
And the most perfect world.

Karen Calverley (12)
Rodborough Technology College, Godalming

79

The Evenstar

(Based on the life and works of John Ronald Reuld Tolkien)

He was the Evenstar who lit the world,
And the hardship of his childhood and the splendour of his tales
Shall never be forgotten.
And ever flowing mix of tongues
Will always be remembered.
And even if the world grows old
And if we forget our past,
The green roots of the ancient trees
Will soon overcome the stone.

A different bed
A different house,
A new world
A strange world,
A heart of fear,
A head of grief.

A single ray of hope
And at the age of 21,
Edith and Tolkien married at last
To pull him from the brink.

A never resting pen in hand
And yes his mind grew weary,
But still he strove and his only fear
Was the look of an unwritten page.

His tales of wonder, hope and fear
And courage of the smallest person
The lights and dreams of men and elves
And the songs they sung in grief.

But now dear Beren and Luthien lie far underground,
And even though now he has passed away into the halls beyond the sea,
We will remember him.

Caleb Jan Rowan (12)
Rodborough Technology College, Godalming

An Inspired Dream

('With a little help from my friends')

It takes an inspired dream . . .

'The quality of mercy is not strained,
One small step for man, one giant leap for mankind,
Hatred can only be overcome by love,
We're more popular than Jesus,
The answer is blowing in the wind.

I will return,
My kingdom for a horse,
Youth is wasted on the young,
Listen to many, speak to a few,
The ballot is stronger than the bullet,

Tiger, tiger burning bright.
The pen is mightier than the sword,
Life is short, but it's the longest thing you'll ever do,
$E = MC$ squared,
I think therefore I am,

Eureka (I've got it!)
There's one born every minute,
Ground control to Major Tom.
Should auld acquaintance be forgot?
Veni, Vida, Vici,

And now for something completely different,
I have a cunning plan.
After all, tomorrow is another day,
Survival of the fittest,
The buck stops here,
It is a far, far better thing that I do than I have ever done',

. . . to change the world!

Harrison Ross (11)
Rodborough Technology College, Godalming

I Have A Dream

Florence Nightingale, oh the kind soul,
Saw the poor soldiers and wanted to help.
So a small group of ladies she got,
And off they went to help all those who were ill.
The middle of the night she was there, the lady with the lamp.

Cleaning, sweeping, helping all,
Making the hospital a better place.
Dirty floors to be cleaned and swept
Florence and her ladies worked hard.
The middle of the night she was there, the lady with the lamp.

Helpless soldiers losing limbs,
Florence was there to help.
Feeding the hungry, cheering up the sad,
Florence could do it all.
The middle of the night she was there, the lady with the lamp.

Thousands of hurt soldiers all needing help,
Florence would help them, every single one.
Wounds kept clean, bones to be fixed
A hard job to keep up, but Florence did.
The middle of the night she was there, the lady with the lamp.

I have a dream, for all to be helped,
Like Florence cared for the soldiers.
For treatment to be carried out quickly like she did,
For hospitals to be kept clean.
She did it with a little help, we have more help so we can do it too.

I have a dream, for us to work together
To help those dying in pain.
Wounds to be kept clean, diseases to be stopped
A big job for us to achieve,
We need to stay determined, like Florence did.

Bethany Dalton (12)
Rodborough Technology College, Godalming

82

I Have A Dream

Think of joyfulness, comfort and safety,
Where you are loved and feel special,
We seem to take so much for granted,
But it's something some people just can't imagine,
They can't imagine being special, or feeling loved.

There are these people in the world,
Beaten and tortured regularly,
This is something I wish to end,
A dream which will never leave,
Unless somebody makes the change in how some live their lives.

Why isn't life fair for everyone?
Those people who are suffering,
Deserve a better life,
Which we are fortunate to get.
Will there ever be an end?

Am I too young to make this change?
Amongst all the people in the world,
If I am, then who will put child abuse to an end?
What can we do? What will we do?
Surely I'm not alone, in what I wish to change.

I dream of everybody able to smile,
To love and accept everyone
Just the way they are and just how they were made
And treat every single person,
As they would like in return.

A message I would give them all -
I would tell them how much they're loved,
There is somebody they shall find,
Who will welcome them just they way they are,
Look forward to this special day a very extraordinary occasion.

Portia Nunn (11)
Rodborough Technology College, Godalming

I Have A Dream

I have a dream,
every night,
of green, green grass,
and gold sun, bright.

A dream of trees,
stretching high,
up into
the big blue sky

A dream of birds,
diving, looping,
always graceful,
gliding, swooping.

A dream of beasts,
playing, jumping,
while hungry others,
are sly while hunting.

A dream of people,
kind and happy,
in no way bad,
not mean or snappy.

A dream of peace,
in a perfect land,
of people happy,
hand in hand.

I have a dream,
every night,
of a perfect world,
bathed in light . . .

. . . but it's only a dream.

Kate Stevenson (11)
Rodborough Technology College, Godalming

I Have A Dream

I have a dream:
to beat the unbeatable,
to conquer the unconquerable
to believe the unbelievable and
to achieve the unachievable.

I have a dream:
to climb the tallest mountain,
to find the most valuable gem,
to buy the priceless item and
to achieve the unachievable.

I have a dream:
to think the unthinkable,
to play the unplayable,
to read the unreadable and
to achieve the unachievable.

I have a dream:
to be able to draw like an artist,
to be able to run like an athlete,
to be able to act like an actress and
to achieve the unachievable.

I have a dream:
to bear the unbearable,
to load the unloadable,
to cure the incurable and
to achieve the unachievable.

Even if I am able to do these things,
two things I definitely want to do are:
to achieve the unachievable
and to live my life as me.

Ella McDuffus (11)
Rodborough Technology College, Godalming

I Had A Dream

I had a dream,
A dream that all poverty will stop in the world,
Forever and ever, never starting again,
All children go to schools,
Have fresh, clean water,
And have the option to do the jobs they wish to do,
I had a dream.

I had a dream,
A dream that ice will stop melting,
And polar bears can be happy forever and ever,
Because they don't deserve to die,
Just so we can live a better life,
I had a dream.

I had a dream,
A dream there will be more heroes in the world,
Like Jack Phillips,
Who risked his life to save others,
Like Mother Theresa,
Who made it her aim to help others,
I had a dream.

I had a dream,
A dream that there are more people in the world,
That stand up for their rights,
Like Martin Luther King,
Who stood up for black people,
Like Emily Pankhurst,
Who stood up for the rights of women,
I had a dream.

A big, big dream.

Megan Gray (11)
Rodborough Technology College, Godalming

What A Sight

Happy and sad
Loved and hated
Remembered and forgotten
Rich and poor

What a sight,
A line of separation,
In every country,
In every nation.

What a sight,
Those with money,
Will spend it all,
Will find it funny.

What a sight,
The poor will clean
All day long,
All is mean.

In the future,
No line of separation,
Just one group,
In every nation.

One day,
Nobody will suffer,
Nobody will be homeless,
But nobody will forget.

One day,
No one will care but you.
When your dream comes true.

Amy Ventress (12)
Rodborough Technology College, Godalming

Imagine A World

Imagine a world
Where children grow with happy faces

Imagine a world
Where a child can sleep without the sounds of battle cries in the background

Imagine a world
Where children are loved for who they are

Imagine a world
Where health care is free for all

Imagine a world
Where food is plenty for all

Imagine a world
Where clean water goes to all inhabitants

Imagine a world
Where children can play freely without fear

Imagine a world
Where every child is equal

Imagine a world
Where every child has a bright future

Imagine a world
Where people don't just imagine

Imagine a world
Where this is implemented.

Praise Gunje (12)
Rodborough Technology College, Godalming

I Have A Dream

I have a dream
That we will fight,
To save the gleam
Of the silvery night.

The crescent moon
Shines down low,
We shall meet our doom
With a steady flow.

The tears you cry
The tears we wept,
You mount to the sky
And never slept.

We gather here
To sign as friends,
Soon we will fear
For the sudden end.

A battle starts
Allies must come,
They read the charts
And are on the run.

It shall be seen
Our friends are curled,
I have a dream,
To save the world.

Jonathan Feasey (13)
Rodborough Technology College, Godalming

I Have A Dream To Stop Animal Cruelty

Animals running, happy, kind.
Running and playing in the park.
Some are tough, some are blind.
If they sense, they whine and bark.

People take them back home.
Leaving them outside the door.
They sit there all alone.
With the touch and feel of their paw.

They feel so left, all so sad
Getting old, hungry and cold.
All these people, cruel and bad
They must be seen, they must be told.

Then a person comes along
They wonder, *what's that?*
Their hearts begin to sing a song
And sit upon the door mat.

The people say, 'Come on dear'
They take them in with them
Feeling no scare, no tear
And cares and treats for them.

They come to a brand new home
When they feel safe, calm and cared for.
They feel like they're not alone
They feel loved again once more.

Kyra Hinton (12)
Rodborough Technology College, Godalming

I Have A Dream

I have a dream
When the world will shine
Things come to life
In a world without strife

I have a dream
When the countries are friends with glee
Wars will be in the past
And peace will come at last

I have a dream
When creatures start to come
Friendships will last forever
And the line of hatred shall sever

I have a dream
When life shall be pure
Like Moses leading people to a land of milk and honey
And the days shall be oh so sunny

I have a dream
When anger and grudges shall disappear
Disgust turns to lust
For a life full of trust

I have a dream
When life is simple
Families stay together
Forever and ever.

David Hasan Hildebrand (12)
Rodborough Technology College, Godalming

I Have A Dream

I have a thought, a wish, a dream,
That life would flow like a stream,
Trickling through pebbles that glimmer and gleam,
I have, I have a dream.

But life's more like a white-water rapid,
With waves, drops and rocks,
Blocking your straight path forwards
With more than just padlocks.

And if you're one of these criminal thieves,
Make us feel alone by all means,
Steal our confidence, steal our fun,
Ruin our lives and block out the sun.

'What have I done to you, why me?'
We ask in the pit of misery,
Our delicate shells shattered, no belief within,
The sadness seeping and creeping in.

We're left there like a voodoo doll,
Needles in our hearts,
The evil deed never fades away,
The beginning never starts.

But if you get freed from the bottle,
Don't let them get in your way
Jump over every waterfall,
And think what a beautiful day.

Edd Keith (11)
Rodborough Technology College, Godalming

In A Perfect World

He has a dream
He stands up for what he believes in
He has a dream
He said that there was hope for black people

He has a dream
He demands freedom and justice
He has a dream
He will continue to believe

He has a dream
He has come to realise the cry
He has a dream
To free the human race from pain

He has a dream
He feels the pain among the world
He has a dream
One voice in one crowd makes a change

He has a dream
For character to shine through us
He has a dream
He wants to change life for others

He has a dream
Dreams can never last too long
He had a dream.

Sophie Levack (12)
Rodborough Technology College, Godalming

The Vision

I have a vision
That one day a child can walk without fear,
They can be free from words that hurt,

Visions that a hand can be shaken instead of it being a weapon,
A vision that I see the day all children smile instead of cry,

Visions that a child can stand up and will not be afraid,
But have the strength to speak up,

Visions that you have tears streaming from your face,
Crying for help but no one is there,
Visions you are screaming out but no one can hear,

Visions of your flesh being newly bruised,
Visions of your body being an unnatural colour but of no fault of your own,

Visions suddenly arrive,
Like a bird flying out from nowhere,
You're not scared,
You're not frightened,
You're happy,
You're saved,

We cannot just have visions,
We need to make visions change,
Transform into reality.

Siân Hine (11)
Rodborough Technology College, Godalming

I Have A Dream

I have a dream
That people of all races and colour
can live in harmony.

I have a dream
That countries at war can live in peace.

I have a dream
That knife crime on our streets will end.

I have a dream
That today all your troubles can be put
behind you so that you can enjoy your life.

I have a dream
That the credit crunch will soon
be over and that people will be able to
afford food and heating
and not be afraid of losing their jobs.

I have a dream
That people living on the streets
will find warmth and shelter, food and water.

I have a dream
That people with ill health will find the
strength to overcome their illness.

Luke Griffen (11)
Rodborough Technology College, Godalming

95

Sorrowful Vision

The ice caps once stood tall and proud,
Glittering in the wintry light.
Now grey, stormy seas just roam around,
No icicles packed up tight.
I had a dream,
A sorrowful vision,
No snowy gleam,
Just melted ice.
Global warming gallops across continents,
Licking thirstily at the diamonds where the polar bears roam.
Electricity means moving forward
But surely this is not what is meant?
We're not making a better world,
But destroying the one we've got.
The ice caps once stood tall and proud,
Glittering in the wintry light,
Now grey, stormy seas just roam around,
No icicles packed up tight
So now I beg, listen to me,
I beg you'll hear my plea.
I have but one more thing to say,
The ice caps are melting,
And so is my heart.

Annie Simons (11)
Rodborough Technology College, Godalming

I Have A Dream

I have a dream,
To help the children,
To save them,
And protect them,

Children need freedom,
So freedom they will get,
More time to play,
And less time doing work,

But in some places,
Children get no work,
Except on a farm or a building site,
So they will get schooling,

Drugs and alcohol,
Gangs and crime,
We must stop this,
And help them live a better life,

I have a dream,
To help the children,
To help them grow up,
And help live a better life,
And help live a better life.

James O'Donnell (12)
Rodborough Technology College, Godalming

I Have A Thought

I have a thought
Something I ponder
Night and day
I twist and turn
Bound in its cruelty
Others writhe
In its path as well

Innocent children
Starve dusk to dawn
Parents too poor to afford education
Some not bothered
Children's eyes
Lose their glow
As unpleasant lives draw near

I have a thought
Will this stop
Will it go on
Should I help
Should another?
Silently still
It creeps on . . .

Emily Canton (12)
Rodborough Technology College, Godalming

I Have A Dream

I have a dream,
To help the poor,
Give them a chance,
Open a new door.

I have a dream,
To feed the homeless,
Take them off the streets,
Stop them being hopeless.

I have a dream,
That war will end,
Their families won't worry,
Their injuries will mend.

I have a dream
That no one will get damaged,
That all the pain will end,
And everyone can manage.

I have a dream,
That peace will come at last,
Everyone happy,
Bullying will be a thing of the past.

Chloe Warner (11)
Rodborough Technology College, Godalming

I Have A Dream . . .

That the world will unite as one.
All hatred will be banished.
Make room for the pure of heart,
Sin no more, only love,
N'ere tread nor step near the darkness
For all hope will disappear.
No more a dream, no more a thought,
No more a world of peace.

Thomas Smillie-Bounds (12)
Rodborough Technology College, Godalming

Barack Obama

Barack Obama, an inspiration to us all,
The first black president to enter the White House hall.
His father left him when he was three,
No one would think he would be:
The President of the USA.

He had no ambition to be in politics,
His dream was to be a writer ever since he was six.
He has two bestselling books,
Read by all different people, even cooks,
These books will stay in history for decades to come.

Going to Kenya to find his father's roots,
Even though being brought up in Hawaii's fruits.
Even though his father had died.
In Kenya he discovered his family on his father's side,
In a village called Alego on the shores of Lake Victoria.

Let's hope Obama will do a better job than Bush
And not drag the UK into any wars at a push.
Help the poor and the homeless too,
And stop racism no matter if they are black or blue.
For the next eight years I'm a supporter of you.

Will Rivington (11)
Rodborough Technology College, Godalming

Dreams

Footsteps down dark winding corridors,
Floating above the cotton wool clouds,
Leaving home in my pyjamas,
Scoring the winning goal.

Falling into a black abyss,
Running through burning searing sand,
Fighting an ever-morphing monster,
These are my dreams.

Jonah Lucas (12)
Rodborough Technology College, Godalming

100

Vera Lynn

During the dark days
When hope is scarce
When tension is building
When soldiers' heads hang down
When victory is out of reach

Inspiration is needed to lighten hearts and souls
To remind them what they are fighting for
To keep them going when times are tough

Bravery needed
Courage needed
Positivity needed

Vera Lynn - an inspiration
A singing sensation
And pride of the nation

Over 60 years on and we are still at war
Over 60 years on and Vera Lynn is still singing
Over 60 years on and she is still an inspiration
Over 60 years on and there are people still fighting
Over 60 years on and the recession is biting.

Ruby Seber (11)
Rodborough Technology College, Godalming

I Have A Dream!

My dream is to overcome global warming,
My dream is to stop poverty all over the world,
My dream is to stop cruelty to children,
My dream is to bring quality treatments to illnesses,
My dream is to make recycling a regular thing for everyone,
My dream is to bring education to every child on the planet,
My dream is to stop all the wars going on around the world,
My dream is to stop bullying
I have a dream to make our world a better place for everyone!

George Watts (12)
Rodborough Technology College, Godalming

Countries Are Quiet

I want peace,
When the word will spread around the world,
And every single person will hear it.

I want peace,
When countries are quiet,
And everybody is happy with what they have.

I want peace,
So people can understand each other,
From around the world.

I want peace,
So people will know,
Who is good and who is bad.

I want peace,
So someone will not cry and cry,
For a lost one.

I want peace
So read this poem,
And think about the words above.

Helena Sharp (12)
Rodborough Technology College, Godalming

My Wish

I wish that everyone could live in peace.
That all over the world there are no wars.
That everyone gets on with their daily lives and there is no trouble.
Everyone getting on with each other.
Sharing, loving each other,
Knowing that they have your trust and you have theirs.
We are not made to create poverty and chaos
But to make the world a better and safer place to live
This is my dream that I want the world to listen to.

Lauren Jordan (12)
Rodborough Technology College, Godalming

Crops Galore

When I dream,
I dream of endless plains,
Of bountiful crops,

Which hold the key,
To end the hunger,
And make weak stronger,

Thoughts still linger,
That it won't remain,
After heavy drought and monsoon rain,

The ravenous sun,
Beams down relentless heat,
And causes crops to wither at our feet,

The whirling winds and howling rain,
Cause an unwelcome symphony,
Of disaster, pain that's this cacophony,

I have a dream that for this harvest,
All shall be joyous and fed,
And not a single tear of mourning shall be shed.

Hayley Toms (13)
Rodborough Technology College, Godalming

My Wish

In my future I wish to stop global warming.
I wish to stop poverty all over the world,
And to help and care for people.
I wish to stop all the wars,
And all the bombs that happen in the world.
I wish to stop cruelty to children
And lock up the criminals on our streets
I wish to stop the stabbings and guns and help those injured
I have a wish that I can do all of these and keep the world safe.

Jack Wilson (12)
Rodborough Technology College, Godalming

A Peaceful World

Just think if there was no abuse or violence.
To stop any actions of feeling of fear,
You don't ruin your life, but you make someone else's better.
And if you think of every consequence, everything matters.
No more bullying would solve 1,000 problems or more.
Because in my dream I saw the world change as one.

Just think if there was no money,
We would live in a world of poverty with fear.
The pleasing sound of laughter, would solve it straight away.
No more war, no more drugs, would again solve at least 1,000 problems.
That would all just fade away.

Just think if there were cures for cancer, for people living in dread.
Then maybe people would think, think about smoking, drugs and more.
But then the world would be at peace, calm yet tired of changes.
And stopping yet starting new dreams.

I have a dream.

Alex Newell (11)
Rodborough Technology College, Godalming

What If?

What if everyone got along?
What if there was clean water for all?
What if the world agreed?
What if poverty ended?
What if there was no more cruelty?
What if there were no more wars?
What if everyone had a good education?
What if there was no more global warming?
What if everyone was equal?
What if . . . What if?

Tom Comben (12)
Rodborough Technology College, Godalming

I Have A Dream

A dream is like the sea
A never-ending land of freedom
A place of free thought
A place where everything is up to us
A dream may be anything or anyone
A dream is a thought from the heart
A dream is something that you see
That no one else can
A dream will stay with you forever
It will slip through your fingers
Then hide, forgotten, in a corner
Until you open your eyes and remember,
That 'I have a dream'
A dream will live always
Though it is forever changing
Living - dying, changing - growing, rising and falling
Until it is lost again
It will disappear to a new home
Or leave when its purpose is fulfilled.

Megan Hurley (11)
Rodborough Technology College, Godalming

My Inspiration

Hands that cannot touch her face
Feet that cannot step a pace
She's never short of joy and delight
Yet she never will have view or sight
She always has enormous hope
And how with odds stacked against her she still can cope
She's a tree of wisdom and knowledge to me
She's my truly inspirational grandma, Elsie.

Chris Waters (11)
Rodborough Technology College, Godalming

105

Untitled

Someone had a dream that all races of people could live in peace,
That poverty will end,
That global warming will not destroy the Earth,
That their children will not be bullied or abused,
That there will be no more cruelty to animals,
And that the poor in Africa will get paid the fair price for their harvest.
People had dreams, but what is important is what is done with those dreams
Martin Luther King helped black and white people get along,
UNICEF is helping poverty in Africa and India,
Childline is helping children through difficult times,
RSPCA are saving animals that have been abused,
Homeless people sell 'The Big Issue' to get money for themselves,
'Fairtrade' is a company that gives the farmers in foreign countries the fair
amount for their food.
However people are still dreaming that they will be able to walk,
That they will have a home to call their own,
That they will have enough food to survive,
That they will not be bullied when they go to school,
And that they could see their parents for one last time.

John De Caestecker (11)
Rodborough Technology College, Godalming

I Have A Dream

I have a dream,
That wars will end forever,
That the world will have peace.
Friends and family will come back,
To loved ones they adore.

I have a dream,
That guns and grenades will disappear,
And no one shall die from them.
To stop trenches being dug,
And to be safe at home.

I have a dream,
To see no wars on the news,
Or soldiers marching with guns.
Have the word 'war' dropped from a dictionary,
And trenches to be filled in.

I have a dream,
That freedom and peace shall be worldwide.

Kiera Ranger (12)
Rodborough Technology College, Godalming

I Have A Dream

Where brown would stick around
Yellow will be mellow
White was right
Imagine if we were in peace
Imagine if we were equals
What if everyone could get along?
I have a dream being cruel
Is not a rule
Instead of drugs sleep in rugs
Most of all education not degeneration
I wish no poverty, just royalty.

Kevin Sibanda (12)
Rodborough Technology College, Godalming

Words That Changed The World

Red is anger
Green is jealousy
This you know better than a book

Purple is violence
Black is cold
This is less commonly known

But to find the good colours
Take a step back away from their lives
The lives of teenagers

Deep behind the pride or hate
There stand the new colours

Yellow is hope
Blue is calm
The one colour that we are the most is white

For it is all the colours that lie in the rainbow
That is what we are made of.

Liam Cole (12)
Rodborough Technology College, Godalming

My Dreams

My dreams,
To give health to all;
My dreams,
To cure global warming;
My dreams,
To educate all children;
My dreams,
To end all wars.
My dreams,
To end poverty;
My dreams,
To cure all from illnesses;
My dreams,
To supply clean water for others;
My dreams,
To stop bullying.
I have my dreams and you have yours,
So let's make them happen.

Alice Jacob (12)
Rodborough Technology College, Godalming

Many People Have Dreams

Many people have dreams
But mine are more like wishes.
They rise and they fall.
Some come true and some fade away
My wish is that all children everywhere
Will get a good education.
My wish is that I will get all I can from life
And live it to the fullest.
To have fun, make friends and lose friends.
Get a good job.
Not to smoke or take harmful drugs.
To set a good example to everyone around me in life.
I know that not everything can come true
But hopefully many things will.
I know that not everyone is perfect,
In fact nobody is,
But whatever happens I will strive to make
My life as perfect as possible.

Poppy Jackson (12)
Rodborough Technology College, Godalming

I Have A Dream

No more wars
I have a dream.

No more pain or suffering
I have a dream.

No more famine or hunger
I have a dream.

No more racial prejudice
I have a dream.

No more pollution or destruction
I have a dream.

No more cancer or illnesses
I have a dream.

No more terrorism
I have a dream.

But it's only a dream.

James Fearon (12)
Rodborough Technology College, Godalming

I Have A Dream

To stop global warming is an important thing,
The planet's concerned, what could it bring?
Poverty increases, crop growth nearly ceases.
Our kids are left to pick up the pieces.

Imagine the end of recession,
Everyone could have a profession.
I hope in the future it's not just the posh,
That earn a good living and have all the dosh.

So now I've decided that this is my theme,
To help end these problems,
Is my true dream!

Freya Bewley (11)
Rodborough Technology College, Godalming

I Have A Dream

A dream is a special thing
Like meeting the big king
You suddenly start to sing
Like a colourful starling

A dream is like a vision
On a big television
You have a commission
To find a little mission

A dream is like a friend
It follows you right to the end
It's something that you can mend
And you can also send

A dream is one big hop
But every dream must stop
The waker is like a cop
Taking your dream with a pop.

Benjamin Ho (11)
Rodborough Technology College, Godalming

I Have A Wish

I have a wish

That racism could be forgotten,
That crimes could be solved.

I have a wish

That all people could be treated the same,
That verbal and physical assault could be stopped.

I have a wish

That the poor and needy could be helped,
That all of the religions, people, could be treated the same.

I have a wish.

Christian Mager (12)
Rodborough Technology College, Godalming

Inspiration

This poem was inspired by my sis,
I think that it's a total miss!
Trying to inspire me was my mum,
But sometimes she is really dumb.

Of course I like my dad,
But his poetry is really sad.
My grandparents are wise,
But they never won a prize.

Nobody could help me,
So I wanted to let it be.
But then my sister came along,
Humming a happy song.

That inspired this bad work.
Yes, she sometimes is a jerk!
But thanks to her I hand this in,
I bet it's going to make the bin!

Alec Neuhaus (12)
Rodborough Technology College, Godalming

I Have A Dream

I have a dream
I want to fly like a bird,
Feel the wind so clean,
Get the bursting bubbles of terror.

I want to be amazed by the sound,
So quiet it will be great.
I'll feel as though the ground is swallowing me up,
The Earth will look flat, not round.

I'll be so close now it'll feel like being in a storm, on a ship's bow.
But I'll be really scared,
What if I . . .?

Ben Starbuck (11)
Rodborough Technology College, Godalming

A Dream Is . . .

A dream is a thought
Of somewhere you've been
Or something you've seen.

A dream is a hope
A fierce desire
Burning away in your belly like fire.

A dream is a want
A need for something near
A passion so sheer.

A dream is a fear
Of something big or hairy
Suddenly it can get very, very scary.

A dream is a moment
When you realise
This is what you want to do.

Oli Hoade (11)
Rodborough Technology College, Godalming

JK Rowling

The way she is kind,
Her books are completely sublime,
The twinkle in her eye,
Like a star in the sky.

She made the book
Harry Potter,
500 pages
It took me ages.

But most of all,
Her heart that cannot fall,
It is so courageous, cunning and brave,
She is just amazing!

Zack Toms (12)
Rodborough Technology College, Godalming

Realisation In A Dream

In my dream she appears to me
Like an angel hovering before the sun
And suddenly I realise that

She's the one
Who keeps me going
She's the one
Who keeps me growing
She's the one
Who gives me knowledge
She's the one
Who I acknowledge
She's the one
Who helps me cope
She's the one
Who brings me hope
My sister.

Elizabeth Rose (11)
Rodborough Technology College, Godalming

Dreams

Dreams
I dream everyone will have fair treatment
Dreams
That one day we will not see the difference between black and white,
Dreams
That around the world we will live together and be treated as equals.
Dreams
Consider a time when no one cares what colour you are.
Dreams
That the whole world will see what was wrong with our old view.
Dreams
Dreams for the future.
I have a dream
A dream of equality.

Jasmine August (12)
Rodborough Technology College, Godalming

My Poem

Click . . . Click . . . Click . . .
Oh why are we faced with TV programs which are bad?
They dull the senses.
Programs about hay and making DIY fences
And cooking shows where they make bad casserole
And fantasy programs with a fake looking troll.

Click . . . Click . . . Click . . .
Again nothing, one of us has to stop these useless programs
Or we shall be faced with
the news on people dying about eating a ham
and people getting swallowed up by a broken dam.
So when you turn on the TV and you see Hugh complaining about
chickens on the TV will you make a sound?

Joshua Perry (12)
Rodborough Technology College, Godalming

A Crime-Free World

I have a dream,
That crime will be no more.
In a crime-free world,
Murder will be a scarcely heard word.
In a crime-free world,
Human kind will flourish.
In a crime-free world,
Peace and prosperity will be ripe.
In a crime-free world,
There will be no wars
For war itself is a crime.
In a crime-free world,
Life will be so much sweeter.
In a crime-free world,
In a crime-free world.

Christopher Brine (12)
Rodborough Technology College, Godalming

Child Abuse

I have a dream
That one day
Children up to your knee
Are safe and snug,
Not bruised by some thug
Who call themselves caring parents.

I have a dream
That child abuse disappears,
Along with the broken bones and hearts,
Of those poor children,
That fathers and mothers don't come home drunk,
And treat their children like some kind of junk.

I have a dream
Let it be known.

Katharine Baxter (11)
Rodborough Technology College, Godalming

Knife Crime

Knife crime, knife crime,
Happening every day,
Killing and hurting,
Many every day.

Families, families
Hurting deep inside
Crying, weeping, praying,
For their lives.

Searching, searching
For a way to stop it
Police and youth clubs
Sorting out the problem.

Claudine Dempsey (13)
St Paul's Catholic College, Sunbury

118

Bullying

As I wake up in the morning
And prepare myself for school
My mind starts to worry
About those girls who break my soul.

As it starts to last all day,
And I can't make them go away
Why bullies don't take a day in my shoes
And feel the unpleasantness they give to you.

My life feels very dark inside
I can't take it any longer
I need to try and be the bigger person
To make myself feel stronger.

As I shared the pain with my mum
I didn't know how to explain it.
It all came out with tears
And my mum was very devastated

She thought I was a happy child
With loads and loads of friends
But when I told her my story
She changed my school in the end

So never let a bully bring you down
And make you not feel strong
Just remember, it's not your fault
They're just jealous, that's all.

Lauren Nichols (13)
St Paul's Catholic College, Sunbury

Depressed

Alone and in pieces,
She feels forgotten like an extinct species.

Isn't she equal to any other human being?
Doesn't feel like it from what she has been seeing,
Insecure or constantly in tears,
On her own to battle her own fears.
No real family to call her own,
Friends that are like family, borrowed with a loan.

Constantly expecting the worst,
Never considered good enough to be the first,
She considered committing suicide,
She had the knife to her heart . . . but couldn't and cried.

Emotionally and mentally dead,
She feels emotionally weak and as if she should be confined to bed,
It is funny the way people assume she is so strong,
When deep down she has been feeling like this for so long.

People only see what she chooses to show,
Only a few really understand the true her and know,
She feels like the diamond in the dirt,
One that has lost its sparkle after being kicked many times
and left hurt.

April-Louise Pennant
St Paul's Catholic College, Sunbury

A Poem About Something Negative

There are a lot of things negative
But not a lot of positive
There are lots of ways to do this
But no one does
We can stop the war and corruption
And stop the anger and distress
That would be a positive world of mine.

Harry Larson (12)
St Paul's Catholic College, Sunbury

I Will Inspire . . .

I will inspire . . .
The kids of this nation
To love and to care for
Our civilisation

I will inspire . . .
The men of this world
To put down their weapons
And let peace hold

I will inspire . . .
To hope and to dream
To live out your fantasy
And never be mean

I have inspired . . .
Myself and my friends
To help each other
And let our hearts mend.

Aaron Byrne
St Paul's Catholic College, Sunbury

Knife Crime

So what's on TV and what's on the news?
I know that everybody has their own views,
It's in every conversation about knife crime
Why can't people stop it from time to time?

When you are walking past that alleyway,
Don't run away and pray,
Don't think that they are going to be fine,
Just pick up the phone and call 999.

Jake Gardener (13)
St Paul's Catholic College, Sunbury

Money

Money, money, you are so great,
Money, money, you cause such hate.
Money, money, you can take us on a ride,
Money, money, because of you so many have died.

Cash, cash, you help the poor,
Cash, cash, with you we start wars.
Cash, cash, you can make impossible believable,
Money, money, you are the root of all evil.

Pedro Takahashi (13)
St Paul's Catholic College, Sunbury

Homeless

I have a dream
That people will hear
The cries and pains of fear
The people among us
Do not all have enough
To buy a train fare
So give a little of your care
To think of all that we own
And those starving to the bone
Weak as a bird that has just hatched
So give them a match
To give a little light
So that they can take flight
Among the darkness of the streets
You can hear their heartbeats
Why should you care
For those who are stripped bare?
They are just like you and me
Hoping for a family.

Kelly Jones (12)
The Marist Senior School, Ascot

On The Stage

Imagine you are on a stage,
With darkness all around you,
When the lights come up you take your spot,
That's where I belong.

I know this might sound
Silly, stupid, lame.
It feels like a dream
A fantasy, a fairy tale,
When I get up onto the stage . . .

. . . I feel like I have a new life,
It feels like I am in a new pair of shoes,
Another set of clothes,
Having a dream is really cool,
But this one I hope will come true.

I know this might sound
Silly, stupid, lame,
It feels like a dream,
A fantasy, a fairy tale,
When I get up onto the stage . . .

. . . You might not like to have the spotlight,
I certainly do, prancing, dancing and acting,
Is my thing.

I know this might sound
Silly, stupid, lame,
It feels like a dream,
A fantasy, a fairy tale,
When I get up onto the stage,
And start to roll.

I will then have found my dream.

Victoria Chessun-Lawrence (11)
The Marist Senior School, Ascot

Sweet Dreams

I was dancing through fields of candy canes
Red and white, multicoloured,
Weaving in and out of lollipop trees.

I looked around at the array of colours in front of me.
All of it tasted sweet.

As I leant forward to smell the popcorn hedges,
A sticky lemon bonbon stuck to my white marzipan frock.
I took the sweets from my marzipan dress
And popped it into my mouth.
I was overwhelmed with the most delicious flavour
That I'd ever tasted:
A marzipan-coated bonbon with a sherbet filling.

I ran over to the ski slopes.
What's different about this? I thought.
I slid down the slope head first with my tongue sticking out.
'Icing!' I exclaimed with delight.

However, I ended up in a sludgy substance with hard bits in it.
After carefully tasting some of this, I discovered with joy
That I was sitting in a world of ice cream and sprinkles.

I sank lower and lower into the ground,
Before hearing a loud ringing in my ear.
I fell through the tub, lower and lower, falling through mid-air,
Before finally I could see nothing.

I turned over and landed with a thud on something painful.

The room then lit up.

'You've been dreaming again! Get up off the floor!' whispered a familiar
voice, 'and you can tidy your room tomorrow! Your sister could hurt herself
on that hairbrush!'

Jess Payne (13)
The Marist Senior School, Ascot

I Have A Dream . . . My Adventure To The Stars

I have a dream
To travel high,
All the way up in the sky.

A gleaming, gorgeous, gigantic world.
There's . . .
Mars
Jupiter
Venus and
Saturn.

A planet that's as cold as ice,
And a planet that has no size,
A star whose temperature rises high,
Like an astronaut in the sky.

A blinding, binding, beautiful sight,
There are . . .
Rockets,
Stars,
Black holes and
Meteorites.

A mind-blowing sight is coming near,
So get on my seat and travel far.

Lucie Singer (11)
The Marist Senior School, Ascot

A Better Place!

I have a dream
To change the Earth
It came to me when
My mother gave birth.

To change war to world peace,
So I decided to tell my niece
She came with me to my lab
She got the phone and called a cab!

She read my plans
Said I'd have lots of fans!
We soon got straight to work
But before long she called her friend Bert!

I yelled at her, 'Get off that phone'
Figure out the angle of the ice cream cone
That night I went to bed
Yet my room stunk of lead!

I went to my niece's in the morn
She was ever so forlorn!
I said to her, 'What's ever so wrong?'
She said, 'This is going to take far too long!'

Fiona Fullilove (12)
The Marist Senior School, Ascot

The Ageing World

My dream is to reverse the damage,
Which we have done to our Earth,
I wish that the trees that stoop,
Like old ladies be lifted with care,
That the rubbish that clutters our streets be removed,
The flowers and plants that look like they are
Scarved with ash from an erupted volcano,
Would be given life and colour,
The river's current which moves,
Like a sloth as it is weighed down with rubbish,
Be drained by a massive sieve so its current moves faster,
The everlasting line of cars,
That spit out fumes like water out of a hose,
Would become environmental cars or even bikes,
That the sunny days I remember which seem not to exist,
As the smog is acting as a blanket tucking away the sun
Be folded up and stored.
That is my dream, do you dream of that too?
Just imagine a gleaming, glistening, glowing Earth once again.

Kaitlin Mitchell (11)
The Marist Senior School, Ascot

127

A Blue And Green World

No disease,
No crime,
No pollution,
A world where happy bells chime.
No wars,
No crowded cities,
No frowns,
Not a world with no pity.
No hunger,
No danger,
No Third World Countries,
Healthy, happy babies asleep in a manger.
I wish the world was fair,
As bright as a million stars.
I wish the world was perfect,
The way God wanted it to be, not full of polluting cars.
In my mind, deep down inside,
I have a dream,
The way the world *could* be.

Millie Stack (12)
The Marist Senior School, Ascot

Changes

I have a dream, when we grow up, things will change.
Many things, trees, houses, planets, stars will rearrange.
The people maybe will be strange.
With begotten robots, doing all our chores,
No poor, no rich, no unhappy, quite a bore.

People will not die; we will not lose the ones we love.
Animals will live together, the kitten and the dove.
We will not look to the God, not pray to the great ones above.
We forget what we live for, dying on the inside.
The children, wonder what our past was like,
How we have survived.

The world today has not been great, but it was not too bad.
I would have been glad, if things stayed the same,
I do not want to be sad.

When we grow up things are going to change.

Megan Viegas (12)
The Marist Senior School, Ascot

I Have A Dream

I have a dream:

H appy birthday actually means something
A ngry parents . . . none of them,
V icious kid across the street . . . gone,
E ven a healthy dinner.

A good night's sleep.

D rugs scarcely known to me
R eal conversations
E ver-loving parents
A new school, new life.
M ummy coming back for me . . .

Will my dream come true?

Tania Nawaz (11)
The Marist Senior School, Ascot

My Dream

I want a good education,
And someone that makes me beam,
I want a happy family,
I have a dream, my dream.

I want to travel the world,
To every place there is to be seen,
I want to have experiences,
I have a dream, my dream.

I want to become a journalist,
Of that I am rather keen,
Or something to do with writing,
I have a dream, my dream.

I want there to be world peace,
Let us all get on like a team,
No more starving, homeless or wars,
I have a dream, my dream.

I have made my family proud,
Or at least that is what it seems,
But I want to make them prouder,
I have a dream, my dream.

I want a lot in the future,
So many things to do and see,
I want to live a really good life,
I have a dream and it's my dream!

Allys Brown (13)
The Sholing Technology College, Southampton

Two Worlds

A nuclear bomb, military precision
A kid in a mask, uninformed decision
The push of a button, two people, one key
AK-47, 'cause they don't agree.

It's so very easy to declare a war
Does anyone really know what it's all for?
Behind a big desk decisions are made
Or a ten-year-old's death disguised with a spade?

Is it power or land or just pure greed
That fills every pore of your body with need?
To fight for what's right, even give up your life
Are their lives really worth it? Your children? Your wife?

Could you justify what you think is right?
Resulting in death in the ultimate fight
The bloodshed and torture, the ultimate shame
Is the death of your enemy the point of the game?

Is there really more meaning than power and lust
When we fight for what we believe is so just?
Who is to say who is right, who is wrong?
Which religion is singing the holiest song?

A lesson well taught through our preacher's eyes
To die for our God is the ultimate prize.

Amy Bewley (14)
The Sholing Technology College, Southampton

Dream Of Hope

Hope that she will see her life through,
Hope that she will stop feeling blue.
Hope that she has the courage to
Continue and thrive and live her life true.

Prayers that she doesn't succumb to pressure,
As if fate has tortured her just to test her.
Prayers that her dreams can live again,
And prayers that she no longer has to pretend.

Dream that she becomes free of the thoughts;
Clouding her head and keeping her caught
In a constant web of demanding questions,
Trapping her mind in confusing reflection.

Please help her, God, if you are there,
To prove to her that we all do care,
So we can realise our dream: to help her,
And that she can live happily, and free forever.

Amen.

Charlotte Saunders (16)
The Sholing Technology College, Southampton

Labelled Cans Of Soup

All blondes are dumb,
They have more fun!
All brunettes are boring,
I am a brunette,
Nobody finds me boring!

I'm not a can of soup,
So why do you give me a label?
I'm not a book
So why do you judge me by my cover?

Annie Bedford (13)
Tolworth Girls' School, Surbiton

Blood's Not Glue

So the world's gone dark,
And you think there's no way out.
The light's switched off,
And you could do without.
Nowhere to turn,
Nowhere to run,
No one who gets it,
No light, no sun.
When the world seems empty,
And your heart is in your toes.
You're screaming inside,
And there's no one who knows.
There are places you can turn,
And people you can tell.
No need to break down,
There's a safe place you can dwell.
The broken need to be fixed,
And blood is not glue.
Self-harming is dangerous,
And preventable too.
Unloved, alone,
Empty and hurt.
Memories that kill,
And a bloodstained shirt.
They just want control,
And it gives you relief.
But is depression and pain,
Your only belief?
Surely you believe in something
And think there must be more.
There's light at the end of the tunnel,
And an opening door.
Us young ones are vulnerable,
And susceptible to pain.
Even though we might act,
Like there's nothing more to gain.
The truth is harsh,
Written on their wrists.
Expressing your distress,

Like nothing exists.
The broken need to be fixed,
And blood is not glue.
Self-harming is dangerous,
And preventable too.

Penny Chapman (14)
Tolworth Girls' School, Surbiton

My Name Is Billy

My name is Billy
I am only three
I don't know what I've done
For this to happen to me.

I have no one to care
Or protect me from him
Shivers surround me
When he walks in.

Mummy's always out
Never here to save me
She thinks he's perfect.
One day she will see.

His fearful punches hurt the most
A bruised leg, a scarred face,
Why am I here?
Such a horrible place.

I can't stop you
Or make you see it's wrong
I just want it to stop
It's been going on too long.

My name is Billy
I am only three
At last the pain has stopped
Mummy can finally see.

Gemma Pavitt (14)
Tolworth Girls' School, Surbiton

RIP Connor

Why did it have to happen
To my best friend?
His life was going so well
And then it all had to end.
We were planning to go out
For the night
But when I got to the park
I was blinded by the light
Police sirens and flashing ambulance
Cars everywhere.
I saw him lying on the floor
I was so scared
My best friend for eleven years
I just wanted to break down into tears.
Blood all over his new white hat,
I was with him yesterday we just bought that.
The police told me he had been stabbed
By a young teen
Was he messed up in the mind?
How could he be so mean?
He had so many plans to be a footballer
When he was older,
It was his ambition and suddenly it was over.
I blame myself, if only I had met him when we arranged,
Maybe things wouldn't have been the same.
So I'm begging you, please, just put down the knives
Because carrying a knife means taking a life.
RIP Connor, gone but not forgotten.
Remember our laughs and the fun times we had.
Best friends forever, I will never forget you.
Look after yourself and remember our saying
Always have hope and never stop praying.

Conee Pearce-Earle (13)
Tolworth Girls' School, Surbiton

136

Fit In The Clique

Size zero is wrong,
Pollutes the minds of the young,
Making themselves thin,
To try and fit in.

They smoke fags,
Hide them in school bags,
Makes them feel full,
To make them look cool.

The next step is drugs,
Dealing with thugs,
Buying some crack,
Snorting some smack.

You're looking gaunt,
You think you can flaunt,
Non-existent curves,
You truly deserve.

You're as thin as a stick,
You're so light I could pick
You up in the air,
Life isn't fair.

Your chances are slim,
You'll meet the Grim,
You better take a vow,
And start eating now.

Being bony is a pity
'Cause curves are very pretty.

Katie Kettle (14)
Tolworth Girls' School, Surbiton

137

Knives Wreck Lives

When things get delinquent,
Don't waste a life.
It isn't remarkable,
To carry a knife.

You may feel immense,
Or think you're almighty on the outside.
But do you really want to risk,
Getting 10 years or more inside?

Black or white
Does it matter?
One life ended,
But others will shatter.

So turn the knife in,
Before someone turns it on you.
Could be a stranger,
Or someone from your crew.

13 years old and carrying a knife,
Now that isn't cool.
Focus on your life,
And doing well in school.

Murdering people does not impress,
It makes your popularity go down less and less
Dash a knife,
And *save a life!*

Abigail Summers (13)
Tolworth Girls' School, Surbiton

Hoodies - Haiku

Big, black and baggy,
Who sees what they are hiding?
Time to stop knife crime.

Emma Smith (13)
Tolworth Girls' School, Surbiton

138

Recycle

Recycle till my home feels greener.
Recycle till I'm eco-friendly.
Recycle till the sky feels brighter.
Recycle all the colours.

Recycle till my arms feel fuller.
Recycle till my ice stops falling.
Recycle till my trees aren't chopped.
Recycle till extinction is extinct.

Recycle till I freeze to the core.
Recycle till I feel excruciatingly hot.
Recycle till I'm safely lukewarm.
Recycle till I regain my breath.

Recycle till the oxygen leaves me.
Recycle till my oceans are clean.
Recycle till my greenhouse disintegrates.
Recycle till the effect is gone.

Recycle till 'they' stop trenching me up.
Recycle till my animals revive.
Recycle while we all construct.
Recycle till they knock my industry down.

Recycle till you realise fate.
Realise I am the Earth.
Dealing with all these things;
Realise not enough people put these things into perspective.

Monica Oluwole (13)
Tolworth Girls' School, Surbiton

Gangs, Knives, Goodbye Lives

Is it my colour? Is it my race?
Why are you holding a knife in my face?
Just one move and it's . . .
Gangs, knives, goodbye lives.

I'm sitting in the park,
You're lurking in the dark,
Get out your knife and it's . . .
Gangs, knives, goodbye lives.

You try to take money,
Threatening me with a knife isn't all that funny,
I don't hand over the money and it's . . .
Gangs, knives, goodbye lives.

I tell you that you should be in school,
You say don't be a fool,
One more word and it's . . .
Gangs, knives, goodbye lives.

You lie in wait,
You only want to show off, show off to your mates,
Anything said and it's . . .
Gangs, knives, goodbye lives.

Nothing done and it's
Gangs, knives,
Goodbye innocent lives.

Hannah Moore (13)
Tolworth Girls' School, Surbiton

Knife Crime

He loved his family
He loved his friends
But over a stupid knife it all had to end.
Intelligent and smart
And with one mistake his life fell apart.

His mum thought it was her fault
For letting him out late
But if he'd done what she had asked
He would have been in by eight.

You don't know who's out there
But most people don't care.

RIP Tom, it's a tragedy you've gone.
We will never forget you
Maybe one day your killer will respect you.

I never thought I'd be standing here
Wiping away my tears
As your coffin goes into the ground
Everyone's quiet; they don't make a sound.

I really wish I could have done something
I miss you mate
From Ollie. X.

Sarah Grafham (13)
Tolworth Girls' School, Surbiton

141

Why Be So Thin?

Why be so thin?
Size 0 is not right!
Don't listen to those fakes.
Don't take notice of what you read in magazines.
You're just too good for that.
So don't be stick-thin and
Have no waist.
So don't listen to those fakes
With no waist
And no taste.
All they want is everyone the same.
Size 0 is not right!
So don't be so tight.
So why be so thin?
It's unhealthy and so gross!
It affects your period and fertility.
So don't let yourself down
And don't be a clown,
With all of the weird styles and sizes.
Size 0 is not right!
Put up a fight.
Take in this advice.
Don't think twice.

Alicia Lawrie (14)
Tolworth Girls' School, Surbiton

To Be Me

I walk into school,
Just through the gate,
And it's nowhere near a ball,
That similar feeling of hate.

I walk into school,
I never really expect much,
There's no point in trying to stand tall,
I only ever get crushed.

I walk into school,
Why are they looking at me?
Am I about to fall?
Why can't they just let me be?

I walk into school,
It starts all over again,
That cruel combat,
Why do they use propane?

I walk into school,
Only next time,
I won't walk to school,
I fear they'll kill me next time.

Kira O'Driscoll (14)
Tolworth Girls' School, Surbiton

Until They Go *Pop!*

Animal testing is wrong,
And I think it should stop.
All the pain they go through,
Until they go *pop!*

It is bad and not good,
It doesn't help at all.
How do we know it will work?
It might affect us all.

Animal testing is wrong,
And I think it should stop.
All the pain they go through
Until they go *pop!*

We force products into their eyes,
Skin, hair and feet.
They go through pain their whole life,
And don't even compete.

Animal testing is wrong,
And I think it should stop.
All the pain they go through,
Until they go *pop!*

Amy Elliott (14)
Tolworth Girls' School, Surbiton

Why Do People Bully Me?

Why, why, oh why?
Why does this have to be me?
I'm just here begging on my knees.
I don't know what I did wrong.

Why, why, oh why
Does this have to be me?
Just because I'm small,
And they're all ten feet tall!

Why, why, oh why
Does this have to be me?
When they hit and when they spit,
It's not something I can quit!

Why, why, oh why
Do they bully me?
I feel depressed and sad,
It really makes me mad!

Why, why, oh why
Does this have to be me?
Why, why, oh why
Do they bully me?

Hayley Marchant (14)
Tolworth Girls' School, Surbiton

Lashes Of My Life

I hid the emotional scars deep within
My mother beat me,
Most of the time with an invisible whip
Made with hurtful words
That cut me deep.

When she thought that I'd suffered enough
She let me go,
I was hoping to escape from this nightmare.

No matter what my age is now,
I am still a frightened girl inside.
As I heard that my mother died,
I hardly cried.

As I watched my mother go underground
I, and the frightened girl inside me,
Knew that today would be a new day.

Even in my old age now,
I still hope that somehow
The little frightened girl inside me
Will soon be free.

Charley Moss (13)
Tolworth Girls' School, Surbiton

Knife Crime Poem

Just imagine waking up
In the morning - picking up the paper
With the words saying
'Another teenager knifed to death.'
How does that make you feel
Upset, sad or even horrified?
That's why you should support the
'Dash A Knife, Save A Life,' campaign
Remember, it could be your friend.

Henna Khan (13)
Tolworth Girls' School, Surbiton

Airport Takeover

We all look at the flowers and the trees,
The woodland critters and bees,
But when the airports get too greedy,
Claiming that they're needy.

These selfish airports are taking land from us,
Laying down concrete and causing a fuss,
Not to mention killing our Earth,
Destroying plants and animal birth,
Soon it will all be gone,
And the airports will be big and strong.

They don't desperately need the space,
But they could tell us to our face,
Instead of buying behind our backs,
Letting us fall through the cracks!

I'm not saying that we shouldn't have holidays,
But show some respect for things we are killing,
After all it will soon be us,
And then we will know how it feels.

Charlotte Anderson (14)
Tolworth Girls' School, Surbiton

Being Different

Out with my aunt,
Having my tea,
I slowly realise
Everyone's staring at me.
They're giving my aunt evils
And they're joking and laughing about my aunt's looks
I think it's best to go,
Before I start to moan and cry,
About how my Auntie's gonna die.

Hope Dear (14)
Tolworth Girls' School, Surbiton

147

Save The Whales

Whales are dying,
In the sea,
All because of,
You and me.

Dumping the oil,
Into their homes,
Killing their families,
Now they're alone.

Why do we kill?
Is it our fault?
We are murderers,
We are killing the whales!

Stop the killing
Stop the pain
Stop this cruelty
Stop it *now!*

Amy O'Brien (13)
Tolworth Girls' School, Surbiton

'Skinnys'

This is my poem, it's about size zeros,
I strongly disagree and they're not all heroes.
They trick young girls to believe it is pretty,
People look up to the skinny girls, it is a pity.
You can see their skeleton, all the bones,
Walking around just looking like clones.
Fitness freaks, work out all day,
They don't know it's bad for them, do they?
Working out for hours is not good for you,
And starving yourself is not good too.
I believe that size zero is really bad,
You should agree; it makes me mad.

Ashleigh Raybould (13)
Tolworth Girls' School, Surbiton

Silence

S cars on my body, scars of silence.
I solating me, trying to break me.
L eaning to punch me, it had to be me.
E ternal torture and pain from my own dad.
N ever talking, never loving me.
C orrupting my life and turning me bad.
E valuate my life from your eyes and try to help me
   I don't want it to be me.

Help me.
I have nowhere to go.
I think I will have to go.
No!
I've had enough and I have to live. I want to.
I need help.
I need to make a call.
I need to break my silence.

Jerina Begum (14)
Tolworth Girls' School, Surbiton

Love

Love . . .
A four letter word . . .
So small . . .
Yet that means *so* much . . .
Everyone's loved . . .
So if you're down and feel alone, be prepared . . .
As your mind will be blown . . .
You're loved
So smile!
Turn that frown upside down!
As we're special in so many ways . . .
You'll be amazed!
Love, love, love!

Lauren Dixon (13)
Tolworth Girls' School, Surbiton

If Only Someone Spoke Up Sooner

Bruises of abuse cover my oppressed body,
Scars of anguish hide deep within my mind,
Leading a life of irrevocable wreck,
Desperate to leave my horrific present behind.

I try to black out the agony they dictate,
The darkness and the sorrow,
I despise the devastation they choose to create.

Being eroded by fear and failing aspiration,
Devours confidence.
Shadows of despair hover over me,
Hopelessly ashamed of my own identity.

I wanted to be heard,
But nobody noticed the distress in my eyes.
If only someone spoke up sooner,
I might still be alive.

Hayley Knowles (14)
Tolworth Girls' School, Surbiton

Stay On Or Dead, Gone

I watch as the burning sun rises,
I watch as the horrific sun dies.
The glowing moon does not help,
The everlasting life is still my living hell
Why will no one stop? I'm ready to drop.
I've lost my pride!
I live in and I live out,
I have been messed around and about.
It would be easier to say goodnight,
Call it a day.
But I might have to pay!
Can I go another time,
Or will I carry on with this rhyme?

Natasha Clegg (14)
Tolworth Girls' School, Surbiton

In Silence I Suffer

In silence I suffer, no shouts and no screams.
In silence I suffer, things get worse in my dreams.
I can't lash out, I can never say no.
I have to obey, I can never let go.
Once there was a mum, who loved me so much,
But since Dad's gone, disaster struck.
I'm thrown and I'm kicked,
I'm hit and I'm cut.
In silence I suffer as I watch days go by.
Locked in my room all I do is cry.
In silence I suffer, I can't escape.
I fear the footsteps that make the house shake.
She's coming, she's here.
What will she do next?
In silence I suffer, as she throws every punch.
In silence I suffer, I just want a lovely mum.

Jessica Hickman (13)
Tolworth Girls' School, Surbiton

Imagine Never Knowing

Innocent lives are being snatched away,
Week by week, day by day.
Animals deserve to live,
They have so much to give.

Imagine existing in their shoes.
Imagine never knowing the life you might lose,
Imagine living only to die,
This immoral testing is enforced - why?

For mascara, for blusher,
For shampoo,
For colour that won't run,
And cream that leaves your skin smooth.

Amy Rengger (13)
Tolworth Girls' School, Surbiton

Am I Different?

As I sit there talking to my friend,
They talk about me and make fun
'Why me?' I ask myself
As I look, they look and laugh
When I answer, they make fun.
Why me?
Why am I so different?
Am I paranoid?
I wish they would stop.
'Why me?' I ask myself,
Why do they laugh at me? What do they get from hurting me?
I wish I could stand up to them.
For some reason, even if I do
I still feel like I will lose everything.
Why me? Why anyone?
So am I different?

Michelle Ranasinghe (14)
Tolworth Girls' School, Surbiton

Fed

Police, police are over there.
These days they're so mean and unfair.
Have you got anything on you?
We can hear them talking about our crew.
We have to move from this place right now
We should go, but how?
The sound of sirens makes my heart thump
Then the car stops and makes me jump.
I hear footsteps, I walk faster
I fall and cut my leg, I need a plaster.
I start to panic about getting in trouble
It's my sister and she bursts my bubble.

Francesca Sweet (13)
Tolworth Girls' School, Surbiton

The Attack

The air is shaking, the Earth is quaking,
The bullets are firing, the sirens are wailing.

Children are crying, people are dying,
For them it's Hell on Earth.

Why does it happen, what has gone wrong?
It's politics and wealth that's mainly the cause.

What about the innocent lives?
The buildings and homes that are destroyed?

Is it fair, is it right?
When will people see the light?

That it's not a solution, it causes more problems.
What is it?
War.

Ammarah Fattani (14)
Tolworth Girls' School, Surbiton

I Know For A Fact

Animal cruelty is still a crime
Five years in jail and a £25 fine
Your four-legged friend
Being treated with neglect and abuse
All for your own entertainment.

Whips, chains and training implements
In the end you're gonna get a punishment.
Snuff films, crush films, pornographic acts
Including pigs, monkeys, hamsters or cats.

You wouldn't do that to me
I know for a fact
If you do it to them
We're gonna *fight back!*

Kaytee Kelly (14)
Tolworth Girls' School, Surbiton

153

Size Zero?

Is size zero,
Really your hero?
Thin, pretty, tall,
Not eating at the mall.
A problem is all you get.

Everyone is different,
So let's keep it that way.
Fat, thin, small,
Whatever makes your day.
Just be yourself
And it might just save your health.

Alice Rushmer (13)
Tolworth Girls' School, Surbiton

Too Busy

Serve and protect,
It's what they're meant to do.
But instead they're looking for benefit thieves,
Taking money from you.

Murderers still out there,
Running free,
Police not looking for them,
Too busy.

Joanna Quinn (13)
Tolworth Girls' School, Surbiton

Dream

The word *dream* means a mystical place
Where our mind rests, the place where
Our thoughts come alive.

The word *dream* symbolises
The magical land where our imagination
Can run free.

The word *dream* brings hope to children
It lets out a cry of pain
Or a sigh of relief.

The word *dream* shows there is hope
In anything, that there is a gleaming glow
In the smallest things.

The word *dream* is big
It is a word full of faith,
A word that makes everyone smile.

The word *dream* to me
Brings hope and joy
It brings me to show
That there is more to life
Than fame and money
That there are people who need a dream
They need a place where their mind can rest
They need that little spark
To lighten up their eyes
They need our hope
They need faith
They need help
They need us!

Chelsea Keen (13)
Westergate Community School, Chichester

The Power Of Dreams

The future is a very big word to me.
For me it's a question, the question is,
What are we going to be when we have finished our education?
Are we going to be reliable, rich, rejected,
Or are we going to reach for our dreams?

There is an old saying, when we want something most,
We will do everything we can to achieve it.
I deeply believe in that phrase and most people do.
My wish is to go to university in America
To play sports and study business.
You may question my difficult dream
But all I can say is, my expectations are high,
And I only live to fulfil.

I personally am a very lively human and instead of being boring
I want to explore the world that surrounds me.
I want to learn from different cultures,
Communities and countries.

If I, an ordinary person, can turn this dream into destiny,
Then I would invest my money for a cure in cancer
And search the open skies for talent
And make that person spread his or her wings.
Everyone's dream is to make life easier,
To stop wars and live in peace and harmony.
I want to make it happen.
Action speaks louder than words
And only an important person can make that happen
I want to be that person in the future.

Mohammed Mustafizur Rahman (13)
Westergate Community School, Chichester

Imagine . . .

Imagine
A world without war.
Peace

Imagine
A world without poverty.
Peace

Imagine
A world without rapists and paedophiles.
Peace

Imagine
That people weren't judged by the colour of their skin
And what they look like.
Peace

Imagine
That cancer was no more.
Peace

Imagine
That one day this could happen

Imagine
One day could it happen . . . ?

Tom Burgess (13)
Westergate Community School, Chichester

I Have A Dream

I have a dream that every child should be happy forever
No child abuse should be used - never!
I have a dream that every child should go to school forever
Free from abuse and neglect forever!
I have a dream that all school should be free from racism and bullying
Because if it is not, the community will be very bad forever!

Devon Arden-Brown (12)
Westergate Community School, Chichester

I Wish . . .

Today, I wish for there to be a change.
No more poverty, hunger or misfortune.
I wish for all our countries to live in peace and harmony.
I wish for there to be a country that judges people by their
Personality, not skin colours.
I wish for there to be a safer community,
Where people don't have to be afraid.

Today, I wish for there to be a change
No more abuse, thugs or terror
I wish for all children to have a good chance in life,
No matter what their parents' wage
I wish for every person to have a home,
To feel warm on a winter's night.

Today, I wish for there to be a change
No more begging, homeless people or starving children
I wish for people to walk through town,
Not being asked for spare change.
I wish for there to be places where the homeless can sleep,
And keep warm.
Not sleeping on a jagged park bench.

Today, I wish for a better world.

Alex Dan (13)
Westergate Community School, Chichester

I Have A Dream

I have a dream
That one day I will meet the queen.
Because I was keen to show her my big machine.
That I will be able to keep the streets clean,
Without being mean to the queen although she is green.

Ellie Harris (13)
Westergate Community School, Chichester

Animals!

People don't seem to care,
What happens to the big brown bear,
The more that die,
Will probably make you cry,

The bats that fly at night,
Won't be there to give us a fright,
If all this pollution,
Continues through our nation,

Mr Mole may be a pest,
When he digs a hole,
But we think he is the best,
So let's save the rest,

The eagle is very shy,
When he soars so high in the sky,
He can see for miles around,
Then he swiftly swoops down to the ground,

So let's stop the gloom,
Look after everything in the bloom,
The animals need to be saved,
We don't need everything paved!

Jessica Myers (12)
Westergate Community School, Chichester

Beat Bullying

Speak up, don't fear
You will be heard here
Victims don't be alarmed
Have the courage to speak up
And you won't be harmed!

Max Page (12)
Westergate Community School, Chichester

I Have A Dream

If we cut down on pollution
The pollution will cut down on us.
The world is coming in closer
And nearly falling to dust.

The nature that Earth grows
Needs to be left alone.
The nature that Earth grows
Needs to be allowed to grow.

The animals that are hurt
And are closer to being extinct
Need to be saved by us
Quicker than we think.

We need to grow
And learn to give
Or we will have
Nowhere to live.

This is my dream
To help the world survive
Together we can bring
These dreams alive.

Paige Irelan-Hill (13)
Westergate Community School, Chichester

My Dream

(This is a true story based on my brother Matt having a bone marrow transplant)

I had a dream that my brother would get better,
Then one day we all got a special letter,
My mum's eyes filled with tears,
As we broke the news to all of our peers,

I was the saviour for my brother Matt,
For doing this I got a brand new cricket bat,
All the needles would come to an end,
They were driving him right round the bend,

I had eighty stabs right into my back,
All the marrow went into a big clear sack
I went to see all the marrow go in,
Instead I was sick straight in the bin,

For being ill Matt got a wish,
As we all slid down the snow in a plastic dish,
A few weeks after Matt got the all-clear,
Then I knew Matt would always be here.

Alex Baker (13)
Westergate Community School, Chichester

Imagine

Imagine
The trees and the leaves will grow again.

Imagine
The butterflies and birds shall fly again.

Imagine
Everything will not die again.

Imagine
The world shall still live again.

Seth Sheppard (12)
Westergate Community School, Chichester

161

Young**Writers**

My Dream

I want to be the girl with
Her name in *lights*

To be the girl who is
Respected by everyone!

To be the girl who will do
Millions for charity!

To be the girl with fame
But a girl who is generous!

To be the girl who makes
People smile!

To be the girl who treats each
Person the same!

To be the girl who is
Independent and successful!

To be the girl who
Is a star!

Izzy Matthews (13)
Westergate Community School, Chichester

I Have This Dream

I have this dream
And will help to make it come true,
It's not right, it's not nice, but it happens.
Children should be able to tell people,
After someone who hurt them has left,
Some don't, some can't and some are just too scared to.
With this dream just imagine all of that
Now that's a dream!
But something should change.

Tiffany Hudson (12)
Westergate Community School, Chichester

162

Anti-Bullying

I believe that bullying is a crime
And as a crime it should be stopped.
It is horrible and violent and vile.

I believe that people should not be treated badly
Just because they are different.
They should not be judged by their size, colour, intelligence
Or the way they look.

I believe that the bully should not get his way
Beating you up and calling you names.
They are just as scared of you as you are of them.

I believe that one day the victims will rise up
Out of the pool of blood and take back what is theirs.
They will stand up to the bullies and leave them in disbelief.

I believe that one day in the future,
The world will be at peace.

. . . And I believe that one day bullying will stop.

Brandon Kingshott (12)
Westergate Community School, Chichester

I Had A Dream!

I come home every night not thinking how lucky I am
I've got a cosy home, they have a cardboard box
I've got a kitchen, all in stock,
They've barely got a box of Coco Pops.
We take things for granted as they have nothing
And the famous people are getting a handful of money
As they're buying new cars and showing off their money
We all have to look back on what we have
As they don't even have a plastic bag.

Chloë Layton (12)
Westergate Community School, Chichester

I Have A Dream

I have a dream
I have a dream to save endangered marine species who face extinction.
Their habitats will be wiped out and destroyed,
Some will perish and others will survive.
When we humans arrive, all the marine creatures will hide.
When the nets sit and wait
All the fish that are caught act as bait.
When the others come swimming they will surely see,
All the little fish dead and hanging in the sea.
What happens next is up to you.
For the disaster that is lying in wait is partly because of you.
So take decisive action and you will surely see
What a difference you could make out at sea.
Do the right thing and speak up now,
Because the future of the sea is in your hands.
It's up to you to make the decision to do what's right
And be amazed by the outcome.

Bryony Jackson (12)
Westergate Community School, Chichester

Every Girl . . .

Every girl has a dream
Of floating down a stream
Thinking about the boy in her dream.

Every girl has a dream
Of eating ice cream
With that special boy in her dream.

Every girl has a dream
Of making a football team
Is this your dream?

Every girl's dream
Is sewn by a seam . . .

Lauren Smith (13)
Westergate Community School, Chichester

My Little Dream

When I was ill I wanted a pet,
But the doctors and nurses said, *not yet*,

Now I've a dog, his name is Ted,
He hides his bones under his bed,

His colour is cream his coat is fluffy,
He's quite timid but really not a toughy,

He sits on the decking watching the world go by,
He also does *sit, paw* and *lie*,

He chases the rabbits but he's too slow,
But the best fun he's had was playing in the snow,

He comes to watch us play football,
He wears a scarf he looks so cool,

Now I've got Ted I've got plenty to do,
It just goes to show that dreams come true!

Matthew Baker (13)
Westergate Community School, Chichester

Everyone Has A Dream!

Everyone has a dream
To be successful, to be seen
To be the one standing there
To love, to care, to share
Everyone has a dream
To be with the one they love
To settle down all lovely and cosy
With your family surrounding
You with love
Everyone has
A
Dream!

Amiee James (12)
Westergate Community School, Chichester

My Dream

My dream is one day that the world will be free from poverty.
Then there will be no need for negativity
My dream is one day that everyone will understand
That black and white people are equal
Then the world will be free from racist people.
My dream is one day that people will understand
That there is no need to start wars.
Then the army won't need to go and kill people anymore.
My dream is one day that people won't be judged by their
appearance.
Therefore will not suffer intolerance.
My dream is one day that everyone will have a home
Somewhere to spend time alone.
My dream is one day that everyone will have a job and proper care.
Which is fair.

Joshua Christian (12)
Westergate Community School, Chichester

I Have A Dream

Imagine
A world without poverty . . . happy or not?

Imagine
A world without paedo's or rapists . . . happy or not?

Imagine
A world with unlimited supplies . . . happy or not?

Imagine
A world without war . . . happy or not?

Imagine
A world where everyone was happy . . .

Imagine
A world where everyone was free to speak out . . . happy or not?

Kurt Stephens (12)
Westergate Community School, Chichester

166

My Dream

To find the cure of cancer one day,
To make the dreams of the victims OK,
To fight the illness that kills all hope,
To save the families that cannot cope,
To help the parents that lose their special child,
To make them laugh when they have barely smiled,
To beat the thing that shows no remorse,
To stop in its tracks the unstoppable force.

This poem is dedicated to the millions of people who
have won or trying to win their fight with cancer but
also to those who have lost someone fighting cancer.
It is also to the millions of people trying to find the cure
for a grotesque and vile disease.

James Baker (13)
Westergate Community School, Chichester

Imagine

Imagine
A world without war
Imagine
A cure for cancer
Imagine
Poor with food
Imagine
A better life for animals
Imagine
A better education for poor kids.
Imagine
For all this to become true.

Bradley Legge (13)
Westergate Community School, Chichester

Football Dream

I dream that one day I will score a goal,
In the big and expensive Archway Bowl,
Going up the steps to get my dream,
My team will be so happy and gleam.

Playing alongside Gerrard, Rooney and Cole,
This memory will always be part of my soul,
So that's my dream, my dream is that,
It's up to me to make it like that.

Jack Bateman (12)
Westergate Community School, Chichester

I Have A Dream

I have a dream
To change the world
To be a team
And be so twirled.

I have a dream
To change the world
To make it clean
And not be curled.

I have a dream
To change the world
To make it green
In a whirl.

I have a dream
To change the world
It's what it seems
To change the world.

Areeba Mehdi (12)
West Lodge First & Middle School, Pinner

Dreams

Dreams can be wonderful,
Dreams can be sad,
Dreams can be happy,
And sometimes very bad.

There are many types of dreams,
They're all around,
Some are adventurous,
Some are fairytales and some are fiction now.

My dream is to make lots of money,
Make my wallet burst with expansion,
Travel around the world three times,
And of course live in a mansion.

We all have different dreams,
Like my friend Sue,
She wants to become a princess,
And live in a mansion too.

Everyone has had a dream
Admit it, even you
Any dream you have had
I hope that it comes true.

Gemini Joshi (11)
West Lodge First & Middle School, Pinner

If I Could

If I could have any dream,
What would it be?
A dream of the sea,
A dream just for me.

The smooth, soft skin,
Of the dorsal fin.
Having this much fun,
In the magic midday sun.

His cute little friendly smile,
Sadly, only stays a while.
Having this much fun,
In the amber afternoon sun.

There swimming all around,
Barely making a sound.
Having this much fun,
In the evolving evening sun.

I wish my dream could go on,
Though it's lasted nearly all day long.
I'll treasure my dream forever,
I won't forget it, ever.

Leaping through the sea,
The special dream just for me.
Having this much fun,
In the special, spectacular, stunning, setting sun.

I dream of a dolphin,
My dream of the sea.

Rebecca Woods (13)
Wood Green School, Witney

I Have A Dream

I tend not to dream most of the time,
as when I do it either results in nightmares or disappointment.
These unconscious hallucinations occur
When I fall into a trap of believing in someone,
Or something that *I* know will bring me pain,
But I continue to believe in it anyway,
We all do it,
But just because we want something to be true,
Makes no difference to the fact that it isn't.

Dreams bring you false hope.
It's actions that have changed the world.
It's actions that *have* made Martin Luther King
the historical figure he is today,
And actions that made Mr Obama the first black president
of the United States of America.

My advice, if asked, would be not to dream,
but to act upon whatever impulse you feel necessary.
Yes, dreams can inspire, motivate and give you confidence.
But what use is a golden bullet when you've no gun to fire it from?

What I'm trying to say is:
Don't stop at dreaming, as you will only find discontentment.
Stop when you have made a dream a reality.
Stop when you can stand and declare that,
You not only have a *dream,*
But that you have your dream.

I have a dream.

Daniella Ashdown (15)
Wychwood School, Oxford

I Have A Dream

I have a dream of no more wars,
No more sieges,
Lots more justice.

I have a dream of more Mother Teresas,
More Florence Nightingales,
Martin Luther Kings.

I have a dream of no starving children,
No street roamers,
Safer streets.

No more illegal drug dealers,
No kidnappers,
No more terrorists.

I have a dream of no more scarred hearts,
No global warming,
No lights left on.

No gas guzzlers,
No landfill,
No garbage-encrusted beaches.

I have a dream of no animal testing,
No more extinction,
No more endangered wildlife.

I have a massive dream,
My biggest dream of all,
Man and creature united.

Francesca Donovan-Brady (11)
Wychwood School, Oxford

She

She walks
She talks

Like you
Like me

She writes
Like anyone else

All together
A family
Appreciation
Love

She sleeps
She stares

With chaos
With fear

She doesn't understand
She's lost

No more time
Lost counting hours
Worsening
Forgot

I forgot.

Aska Matsunaga (15)
Wychwood School, Oxford

I Have A Dream

I have a dream,
Of a caring world,
Of a world full of justice,
A fair world.

I have a dream,
Of a road full of smiles,
Of a playground of laughter,
A happy world.

I have a dream,
Of educated children,
Of black and white children together,
An equal world.

I have a dream,
Of a fighting-free world,
Of no guns for killing,
A peaceful world.

I have a dream,
Of a world with no slaves,
Of no blackmail,
A free world.

Rozhin Tajermanshadi (11)
Wychwood School, Oxford

I Have A Dream

I have a dream,
Make the world fair,
No war, evil or madness,
Justice!
Peace in the world,
Stop the greed.

I have a dream,
Make the world fair,
No knives, guns or bombs,
Justice!
War must stop,
Fights must stop too.

I have a dream,
Make the world fair,
No racism or sexism,
Justice!
Treat everyone the same,
Make people happy again.

This is my dream!

Louise Pollard (11)
Wychwood School, Oxford

I Have A Dream

I have a dream
That when I wake up,
Black and white
Will drink from one cup

I have a dream
When I look out the window,
I will not see a beggar
Or a poor grieving widow

I have a dream
That when I read the news,
There will be no stealing
And no one abused

'I have a dream,'
Said Martin Luther King
That the world will be put right.
Everything.

Annabelle Ashdown (11)
Wychwood School, Oxford

I Have A Dream

I have a dream that all people are equal,
I have a dream where no people die,
I have a dream that everyone is a family.

I have a dream for a perfect life,
I have a dream for all good and strong,
I have a dream for no bad or wrong.

I have a dream that all is healthy,
I have a dream that all have clean water,
I have a dream that no one is poor.

Jessica Clews (11)
Wychwood School, Oxford

A Natural Dream

I have a dream:
Of birds flying out of cages,
Of flowers blooming freely,
Of all road travel by horses.

I have a dream:
That instead of driving cars
Everyone rides, bikes or walks,
Everything is eco-friendly.

I have a dream:
Of no world destroyers,
Of clean energy and windmills,
Of all caring for nature.

I have a dream.

Charlotte Gye (12)
Wychwood School, Oxford

Young Writers Information

We hope you have enjoyed reading this
book - and that you will continue to enjoy it
in the coming years.

If you like reading and writing poetry drop
us a line, or give us a call, and we'll send
you a free information pack.

Alternatively if you would like to order further
copies of this book or any of our other titles,
then please give us a call or log onto our
website at www.youngwriters.co.uk

Young Writers Information
Remus House
Coltsfoot Drive
Peterborough
PE2 9JX
(01733) 890066